THE HEALING MINISTRY OF JESUS CHRIST CONTINUING IN THE CHURCH TODAY

Father Peter B. Coughlin, D. Min.

THE HEALING MINISTRY OF JESUS CHRIST CONTINUING IN THE CHURCH TODAY

Published by:

C.C.S.O. Bread of Life Renewal Centre
P.O. Box 395
Hamilton, ON   L8N 3H8 Canada

www.thebreadoflife.ca

Cover Art by Cesia Piotrowski

ISBN 0-9683966-6-6

Printed in Canada by:

The Ave Maria Centre for Peace
Toronto, ON   Canada

... They will lay hands on the sick and the sick will be healed (Mark 16:18).

I dedicate this book to all who down through the centuries have had the courage to reach out and bring the Lord's healing touch to those in need. Some have ministered healing as a special charism in an extraordinary way. Others have reacted to the need before them by simply asking Jesus to heal their loved ones. It is through the Charismatic Renewal in our own times that healing has been restored to regular ministry in many parishes through people who have been empowered by the grace of the Holy Spirit. May the healing ministry of Jesus Christ become more and more evident in this world that so greatly needs the saving love of God to become whole. Every person who has faith in Jesus Christ knows that He is the only healer, and through expectant faith and the empowerment of the Holy Spirit the healing ministry of Jesus Christ continues in the Church and the world today.

This book has been my doctoral project for the Doctor of Ministry degree obtained from the Graduate Theological Foundation in Donaldson, Indiana. It also reflects over thirty years of study and experience in the healing ministry of Jesus Christ.

The Lord has given me a great gift in the person of Timeena Cervoni, a dedicated and willing volunteer with great skill, whose expertise has taken my handwritten text and brought it into full book form. Not being typewriter or computer literate, I fully appreciate the talent and gift of Timeena who has given countless hours to editing, typing and formatting all that needs to be done to bring this work to completion. I pray God's abundant blessings upon her and her family.

Special thanks also to Cesia Piotrowski who completed a labour of love to bring to birth the cover art for this book in order to convey the book's content.

Table of Contents

INTRODUCTION

Thirty years of healing ministry prayer have taught me much about the healing ministry of Christ Jesus and the struggle that many Christians have to understand and accept that Jesus does heal today. Jesus is the Healer. I am not. I simply pray and ask in faith. Jesus heals both directly and indirectly, through the official prayers of the Church and through individuals who turn to Him with expectant faith in prayer for their needs to be met. God heals in the name or person of Jesus through the power of the Holy Spirit.

When we read the Bible – especially the Gospels and The Acts of the Apostles – and the history of the Church, we see Jesus as The Healer who sets people free, makes them whole, restores them to life, and hands on to His apostles and the disciples the same authority and power of the Spirit to do the same and even greater works than He did. Jesus is the Man of the Spirit, filled to the fullest measure with the presence and power of the Holy Spirit through whom Jesus lived, died and rose again, as He carried on His ministry of healing and setting people free. In Acts 10:38 we read: "God had anointed him with the Holy Spirit and with power, and because God was with him, Jesus went about doing good and curing all who had fallen into the power of the devil."

The Church by the power of the Holy Spirit carries on the ministry of healing through the administration of the sacraments, especially the Anointing of the Sick, and through the charisms of the Holy Spirit. The Spirit is alive and active within the Church, enlivening not only the institution but also the members of the Church. Healing involves loving and forgiving. Healing is wholeness of the total person and his environment, deliverance from demonic power and influence,

i

forgiveness of sin and life from death.

Down through the centuries, divine healing has been approached in different ways by different people. One way would be confrontational, breaking the hold of the evil one over a person to set them free and restore them. Another is intercessory, appealing directly to the Lord or through one of the saints or a holy person that healing may take place. Another is incubational in which a person stays and prays in a shrine or a retreat centre until they receive healing. The reliquarial method would be to use relics of the saints as touchstones to be in direct contact with a saint or holy person who has died, expecting that the prayer to the person would be effective. A revelational approach is one in which a person receives from the Lord a revelation of the healing taking place and speaks it to the person or persons who then receive the anointing touch of God upon their lives and so healing takes place. The soteriological approach is to call and invite people to embrace the cross to crucify their sinful passions and desires, receiving salvation, the healing effect of salvation won for us by Jesus Christ through His death and rising from the dead.

Through baptism and the empowerment of the Holy Spirit we are called to be followers of Jesus, formed to be disciples who exercise the charisms in ministry of service. The charisms are the passing manifestations of the Spirit in the moment to meet specific needs, to bring miracle, healing, freedom, wisdom, knowledge, discernment, blessing and encouragement, the revelation of the Lord's word, mind and heart, to a given situation or circumstance. To minister in the power of the Spirit is a normal part of Christian living.

Divine healing is not faith healing. Healing does not depend solely on having enough faith to be healed. Healing involves the will of God, a climate of faith and readiness to receive. Today the preaching of healing and deliverance creates a climate that awakens faith and expectancy that God does and will give healing. So often the biggest difficulty in receiving healing is for the person to take their eyes off the problem or the infirmity and give the Lord full attention and permission to do the healing needed. It really is a matter of asking and receiving. That may well require giving forgiveness, having a forgiving heart and being free from sin and negativity, having one's heart open to receiving God's gift as one asks in the person of Jesus. Trusting in God's power and establishing a relationship with Jesus, people open themselves to whatever the Lord in His compassion and power would do for them. In a lived relationship with Jesus, healings occur to lead to or strengthen that relationship.

Throughout Church history God has intervened to bring restoration to health by His direct intervention. Divine healing continues today as it did when Jesus ministered healing in Galilee wherever He travelled. Jesus never ministered healing in one particular way nor did He give any particular formula or prayer to use to bring about healing. Jesus is the healer and how it is accomplished is a mystery. Healing is all about God's unconditional and unending love freely given to whomever He chooses. Divine healing takes place in a person's experience, but it is God who brings it about through the power of the Holy Spirit.

What is the healing ministry? It is God's love made real, tangible through the Lord's direct or indirect ministry as He intervenes to make new, renew and transform the circumstance of His beloved people.

Prayer for healing is the cry of the heart for Jesus to act, to restore, to heal or set free one's self or another. We approach the Lord with humility and simplicity in our limitations and vulnerability, in our weakness, poverty and need. Jesus has the authority. Jesus has the power to heal through the Holy Spirit. As disciples of Jesus we have been given authority by Jesus and through the power of the Spirit present in us we minister healing, the loving touch of Jesus

Christ the Healer.

Healing is an ongoing process whereas a cure means that the difficulty has been completely dealt with. Healing is always necessary and comes in a variety of ways as a person is brought to wholeness. God intervenes directly to bring wholeness to the individual. Healing is God's work in the life of an individual. We know the prayer for healing is answered when the pain disappears, movement is restored, symptoms of illness disappear, the person knows peace; fear is gone; life, energy, vitality is restored and joy, wonder and awe at God's goodness is experienced.

Stories abound of the healing action of Jesus in countries of the Third World. Fewer stories are told in the more prosperous nations because of the lack of faith, complacency or unwillingness to change or to grow in relationship with Christ. Faith and expectation of God's action are so necessary. The ministry of Jesus focussed on preaching the kingdom and making disciples. When Jesus leaves Capernaum and travels throughout Galilee He says to His disciples, "'Let us go elsewhere, to the neighbouring country towns, so that I can preach there, too, because that is why I came.' And he went all through Galilee, preaching in their synagogues and casting out devils" (Mark 1:38-39). Jesus teaches the necessity of faith and the importance of prayer as a priority in one's life. He helps people grow in faith and He confronts the prevailing climate of unbelief. He saw His own ministry of healing and deliverance as evidence that He is the Messiah.

The Church continues the mission of Jesus guided, empowered, led by the Holy Spirit. Countless disciples throughout the centuries minister in the name of Jesus Christ, continuing His healing ministry.

When I see the people in my parish I see that every single one of them has a need for healing, whether it is spiritual, medical, emotional, psychological or relational. How do we offer to people in the parish the experience of the healing ministry of Jesus Christ? It doesn't only occur in the Sacrament of the Anointing of the Sick but also in a whole variety of ways as the Lord answers the prayer of those who turn to Him. In our parishes everyone needs to be formed or discipled in ministry to the sick.

This book explores the healing ministry, prayer for healing, the Scriptural foundations revealing the practice of Jesus and His disciples. Looking at the sacraments of healing, their pastoral applications and day-to-day experience of divine healing, various practical procedures are given for different ministry forms. Also, possible dangers, abuses and aberrations in healing ministry are presented together with answers to regularly asked questions about healing. The final chapter looks at the challenge and place of healing in evangelization today.

This book is being published particularly for the Catholic Church to encourage expectant faith and the empowerment of people to pray in Jesus' name for healing, with wondrous results.

Rev. Peter B. Goughlin

Chapter 1

WHAT IS THE HEALING MINISTRY?

What is the healing ministry? No one really doubts the need for healing in their own life or in the lives of others. Today, healing is a marketable product as seen in the rising trend of health food stores, natural medicine, the use of herbs, organically grown foods, and the ever-increasing use of drugs. Society is focused on eradicating disease of all kinds. Even on television, products are marketed and healing through the Divine is offered by television evangelists. Healing is important and, indeed, even necessary, if life is to be lived free of pain, infirmity and disease.

Medical science is continually developing new methods to combat disease and there is a strong reliance on surgery and drugs to deal with the presenting problem. Every person I know has a need for healing in some way, whether of mind or body, emotions or spirit, in their relationships or life circumstances. It is my experience that many people try many different ways or means offered to find peace, balance, wholeness in their lives. And many of these same people do not recognize that they can receive healing, wholeness, peace, freedom, right balance from Jesus Christ who continues His healing ministry in the Church today.

Healing is real and is attainable. A doctor can treat but only God can heal. God heals in the name of Jesus through the power of the Holy Spirit. When we read the Bible, especially the Gospels and The Acts of the Apostles, we see Jesus as The Healer who sets people free, makes them whole, restores them to life, and hands on to His apostles and the disciples the same authority and power of the Spirit to do the same and even greater works than He did.

Jesus is the Man of the Spirit, filled to the fullest

1

measure with the presence and power of the Holy Spirit through whom Jesus lived, died and rose again, as He carried on His ministry of healing and setting people free. So often we can tend to focus on the teaching and preaching of Jesus but that was only part of His ministry. Primarily, He was a healer who broke the devil's power: "God had anointed him with the Holy Spirit and with power, and because God was with him, Jesus went about doing good and curing all who had fallen into the power of the devil" (Acts 10:38).

The Church by the power of the Holy Spirit carries on the ministry of healing through the administration of the sacraments, especially the Anointing of the Sick, and through the charisms of the Holy Spirit. Bishops share with priests the privilege and responsibility of bringing Jesus to the people. This is done by preaching, teaching and example, but also through the sacraments, moments of encounter with the Risen Jesus which are meant to focus, change, transform and renew those who receive them. Pastoral care of the people involves establishing them as sons and daughters of the Father, brothers and sisters of Christ Jesus and as companions of the Holy Spirit who carries on the mission of Jesus to renew all of creation. Through initiation into the Church as disciples of Jesus filled with the Spirit we do the same works to bring healing and wholeness, forgiveness and peace.

Called to be followers of Jesus, we are formed as disciples who exercise the charisms in ministry of service. The charisms are the passing manifestations of the Spirit in the moment to meet specific needs, to bring miracle, healing, freedom, wisdom, knowledge, discernment, blessing and encouragement, the revelation of the Lord's word, mind and heart, to a given situation or circumstance. To minister in the power of the Spirit is a normal part of Christian living. The Church is both charismatic and institutional, the one not able to exist without the other. The Spirit is alive and active within the Church or else the institution would be dead. The Spirit is the very soul of the Church enlivening and ministering through its members. The Spirit's purpose is to make holy the Church and the members of the Church as the Spirit reveals Jesus who glorifies the Father.

Healing involves loving and forgiving. Healing is wholeness of the total person and his environment, deliverance from demonic power and influence, forgiveness of sin and life from death. Healing is sharing God's abundance with the oppressed poor. Healing is growing in community, in the Kingdom of God. Healing, wholeness and holiness are touching, receiving God's mercy. It is divine love being ministered. Healing is embracing salvation, applying the merits of the cross to pain and suffering. Healing is real! It happens! God's desire is for our blessing, strengthening, wholeness and holiness. Through faith and prayer God's will is revealed and embraced, hearts are turned towards the Lord and the presence and power of the Spirit are manifested to meet us in our daily needs to be forgiven, restored and brought into right order and relationship so that the peace and holiness of the Lord Jesus fills our lives.

Down through the centuries divine healing has been approached in different ways by different people. One way would be confrontational, breaking the hold of the evil one over a person to set them free and restore them. Another is intercessory, appealing directly to the Lord or through one of the saints or a holy person that healing may take place. Another is incubational in which a person stays and prays in a shrine or a retreat centre until they receive healing. The reliquarial method would be to use relics of the saints as touchstones to be in direct contact with a saint or holy person who has died, expecting that the prayer to the person would be effective. A revelational approach is one in which a person receives from the Lord a revelation of the healing taking place and speaks it to the person or persons who then receive the anointing touch of God upon their lives and so healing takes

3

place. The soteriological approach is to call and invite people to embrace the cross to crucify their sinful passions and desires, receiving salvation, the healing effect of salvation won for us by Jesus Christ through His death and rising from the dead.

Divine healing is not faith healing. Healing does not depend solely on having enough faith to be healed. Healing involves the will of God, a climate of faith and readiness to receive. Today the preaching of healing and deliverance creates a climate that awakens faith and expectancy that God does and will give healing. So often the biggest difficulty in receiving healing is for the person to take their eyes off the problem or the infirmity and give the Lord full attention and permission to do the healing needed. It really is a matter of asking and receiving. That may well require giving forgiveness, having a forgiving heart and being free from sin and negativity, having one's heart open to receiving God's gift as one asks in the person of Jesus. Trusting in God's power and establishing a relationship with Jesus, people open themselves to whatever the Lord in His compassion and power would do for them. In a lived relationship with Jesus, healings occur to lead to or strengthen that relationship.

Throughout Church history God has intervened to bring restoration to health by His direct intervention. Divine healing continues today as it did when Jesus ministered healing in Galilee wherever He travelled. Jesus never ministered healing in one particular way nor did He give any particular formula or prayer to use to bring about healing. Jesus is the healer and how it is accomplished is a mystery. Healing is all about God's unconditional and unending love freely given to whomever He chooses. Divine healing takes place in a person's experience, but it is God who brings it about through the power of the Holy Spirit.

The gift of healing belongs to the one who receives healing from Jesus. The ministry of healing is exercised by whomever the Holy Spirit uses for the manifestation of His presence and power. A person who is willing, says "yes" to being empowered for ministry and exercises the courage needed to act in a particular need can be said to have the ministry of healing when their prayers are regularly answered. A person may be used to bring healing once or countless times. One really knows they have a ministry of healing when people keep knocking on the door for them to pray for healing. In my own life I have been exercising a healing ministry for over thirty years.

Some people are specialists when it comes to prayer for healing, for example, being effective in prayer for back problems or with cancer patients, for healing of memories of soul-spirit hurts, in healing of open wounds or relationship difficulties. For myself, I consider myself more of a general practitioner in that I pray for everything and often see amazing healings or miracles take place. All people are to pray for healing for self and others but some are gifted with an extraordinary ministry of healing to the sick.

There are many questions that surround the healing ministry. Does everyone get healed? I firmly believe that healing occurs every time we pray for it, but it may not be the healing for which we specifically ask. The Lord knows what is for our greatest good and blessing. For example, we might pray for a specific physical healing and the healing received is the absence of fear or anxiety, an infilling of peace, or a different physical need may be met. The Lord reveals His presence and power in order to deepen our relationship with Him, form in us holiness, strengthen our faith or simply to delight our spirits – filling us with joy and greater love for Him.

Healing may happen immediately or it may come slowly by stages. All healing is from Jesus and He knows the best way for us to grow strong in Him. We marvel when pain instantly disappears, when a person has free movement, hearing or sight restored, the heart changed or transformed. Instant healings help to increase the sense of expectancy in faith for other healings to be received.

Sickness and death come about in the lives of all of us because of the effects of the original sin of our first parents. That does not mean that an individual sickness is caused by the person's own sin or the sin of their parents. Sickness and death are part of the human condition because of our fallen human nature. There are good and holy people who suffer unrelieved sickness, poor health, weakness, and do not get well. This is part of the mystery of divine healing and God's will and purpose. It may be that the infirmity keeps the person in relationship with the Lord or deepens the relationship. Their situation may bring faith to others and be a testimony as to how a Christian deals with suffering through faith and dependence on the Lord.

I remember a young man of twenty-seven dying of cancer who was a great example to all on the hospital floor though he was not a church-goer. When people asked or lamented how this could happen to him, he responded, "Why not me?" In another situation I was asked to see a man with whom I had prayed fourteen years before. Unknown to me he was instantly healed of brain cancer when I had prayed with him. Fourteen years later I was told this. Cancer had recurred and I prayed with him again. I knew when I prayed that he would die in two weeks' time. However, the healing that took place this time was in his spirit. He forgave and reconciled with his brothers and his sons and had a wondrous and peaceful death with his family and both parish priests at his bedside. What he had not made right the first time he received healing, he accomplished before his death, dying a happy man ready to meet the Lord. In another situation I prayed with a woman in great pain after surgery for cancer of the spine. She had also wrenched her knee and pulled a muscle in the opposite thigh and needed a lot of help to move about. When

I prayed with her, her knee was healed instantly and all the pain disappeared. She remained pain-free until two days before her death several weeks later when she died happily and at peace.

Believers don't always get well. Their ministry is often found in their witness of how to live in the midst of sickness and suffering. And healing accompanies their faith as their spirits are made whole and holiness becomes more and more evident in them.

Medicine, too, is God's gift and doctors and pharmacists work for healing in the lives of the people they serve. When the Lord heals, it is good to seek confirmation from the doctor and let the doctor terminate the medication that has been prescribed. When a person receives divine healing, they know they have been touched by God, set free and healed, made new in the wonder of divine love.

What is the healing ministry? It is God's love made real, tangible through the Lord's direct or indirect ministry as He intervenes to make new, renew and transform the circumstance of His beloved people.

Chapter 2

PRAYER FOR HEALING

People tend to look for the prayer that works, the formula that will bring about healing, change the circumstance, take away the pain, restore health and vitality. But there is no one prayer that works. There is no magic formula. There are so many different illnesses, infirmities and ways in which people are held in bondage. People get overwhelmed by fear and anxiety, worry and doubt. They can be inclined to "try" this or that, wanting something that "works" to put things back the way they were or that makes them better.

Prayer for healing is the cry of the heart for Jesus to act, to restore, to heal or set free one's self or another. We approach the Lord with humility and simplicity in our limitations and vulnerability, in our weakness, poverty and need. Jesus has the authority. Jesus has the power to heal through the Holy Spirit. As disciples of Jesus we have been given authority by Jesus and through the power of the Spirit present in us we minister healing, the loving touch of Jesus Christ the Healer.

By myself, my own words or actions, I have no power to heal anyone. I pray. Only Jesus can heal. Knowing that He is God and I am not, I can approach Him with the simple prayer of my heart, aloud or silently, formally or spontaneously, asking for healing, wholeness, holiness. A simple prayer is best. It doesn't need to be long or complicated or attentive to every detail. But the prayer invites and gives the Lord freedom to act without telling Him when or how or through whom He is to do so. Neither do we tell Him why or where He is to do so. The Lord is sovereign and how He acts for our greatest good, our welfare, is entirely up to Him. We propose and God disposes.

Often, when I have offered to pray with someone for healing the response is, "You can pray for me, not with me" or "I just need to rest" or "I'll just take an aspirin" or "It's all right. It'll get better." So many seem to be afraid of the power of God, that they are not worthy, don't want to bother the Lord, or that the Lord isn't interested. It is amazing how people adjust to their circumstances even when they don't want to bear the pain or the limitation or the sickness. They limp but keep on walking.

In praying for healing with an individual or a group I encourage taking one's eyes off the problem and focussing on the Lord, giving Him permission to do the healing. Then I ask that those receiving prayer just simply be aware of the Lord's presence and not to pray but just receive the Lord's healing touch in their lives. The climate of faith is so important, that there be an expectancy of the Lord's action and response. Healing doesn't depend on the individual's faith. The Lord may heal in order to give faith. For example, I remember a man coming to a Mass for Healing not believing in the possibility of healing. He had been "trapped" into coming. By the end of the evening he couldn't understand how all his bursitis had totally disappeared from his arm and shoulder when he didn't believe such a thing could happen. Jesus had healed him and he came to have faith that Jesus does heal.

We have probably all heard stories of people who turned to the Lord in their desperation and the Lord sovereignly acted to heal. The recipients of His healing basically told the Lord they couldn't take it any more or they simply told the Lord they couldn't do it and asked Him to act. Jesus did and healing took place, the heart changed, the person was set free or made new, transformed by the miracle of God's grace.

Sometimes people persevere in prayer for a long time before they experience God's answer to prayer. The answer comes when they let go and let God. It comes when the purpose for the sickness or infirmity has been accomplished. The person takes steps to correct a situation or accepts their circumstance, taking their eyes off the problem and placing them on Jesus. The heart changes, the person recognizes the hidden blessing, lets go of control, learns to laugh at self or circumstances, embraces virtue and becomes a witness to Jesus Christ.

Many struggle with stress on a daily basis, get burned out by losing their vision or the Lord's vision and get depressed, lose hope and joy. To find stability, peace, right order and values, one must be careful of negativity and self-depreciation and reach out to embrace the God who heals. Some are not healed in the way they ask. But in my experience, when we ask, healing always takes place in some way. It may be by having the fear or anxiety simply disappear, being filled with peace, having a new understanding of the meaning and purpose for this particular condition. It may be renewed courage, hope or confidence and trust in the Lord to provide. It may be healing of the inner spirit of a person or in a deepening appreciation of the Lord and His love and self-sacrifice. It could be in the recognition of the eternal value of suffering, of using the way of suffering to give witness and to build up the kingdom of God. A person always has the opportunity and the possibility of real spiritual growth and inner strength being developed through their suffering, a suffering that can be used to benefit others.

Everyone wants the highest quality of life, to live abundantly, have excellent health, the resources to live a wonderful life and the freedom to take advantage of the good thing, the blessings life offers. When we get ill or infirm we want to get well as quickly as possible. Persistent sin, wrong relationships or life-style, lack of repentance or forgiveness, unwillingness to turn to the Lord for healing can be reasons why some are not healed. But it may simply be God's will that now is not the time for the healing to be complete, that another divine purpose is at work in our lives. Our lives are full of mystery when it comes to God and His ways. Life and death are full of mystery. Healing and suffering are also full of mystery. No matter how we try to explain mystery, there are elements beyond our comprehension; and no matter how much we try to solve the incomprehensible, we are to seek the God of the incomprehensible for healing and peace.

In the gospels we read that Jesus was approached by large numbers of the sick either directly or through relatives and friends seeking the restoration of health. Jesus generously deals with every request, granting healing and restoration. Trusting prayer or intercession offered to God in Jesus brings wondrous results. In the book of Ecclesiasticus, Sirach exhorts his disciple, "My son, when you are ill, do not be depressed, but pray to the Lord and he will heal you" (Ecclesiasticus 38:9). In fact, the first fifteen verses of chapter thirty-eight speak wonderfully of medicine and illness, of turning to the Lord for healing but also relying on the doctor and the pharmacist through whom the Lord works. The psalmist expresses his desire for healing and offers prayer to obtain relief from his distress, help in time of trouble, in sickness and suffering (cf. Psalm 6; 38; 41; 88). God is faithful to hear and answer. In First Chronicles 4:10 we find a testimony of God who answers prayer: "Jabez called on the God of Israel. 'If you truly bless me,' he said, 'you will extend my lands, your hand will be with me, you will keep harm away and my distress will cease.' God granted him what he had asked."

Sometimes it seems that we are always asking God for healing or blessing in a great variety of needs. Yet, the Lord hears us and is with us in our times of need as He is at all times. It seems that we become more anxious or desperate for His intervention when the problem is too large to deal with by one's self. And so people turn in desperation to the Lord but their focus is often on the problem, not on the Lord. Every person I have ever met has some need for healing. It is a wonderful thing for an individual to ask for healing for themselves or others. Even the Church continuously offers prayer for healing for her members in every Mass, through the sacraments, in the use of sacramentals, at shrines and holy places, and in specific services of prayer for healing. Those who gather for daily or weekly Mass pray for the sick, for healing, every time the general intercessions are offered.

Specifically, one of the sacraments, the Anointing of the Sick, is ministered to the sick to strengthen, heal, restore and forgive the sins of those who need the Lord's forgiveness. The apostle James wrote,

> If any one of you is in trouble, he should pray; if anyone is feeling happy, he should sing a psalm. If one of you is ill, he should send for the elders of the church, and they must anoint him with oil in the name of the Lord and pray over him. The prayer of faith will save the sick man and the Lord will raise him up again; and if he has committed any sins, he will be forgiven (James 5:13-15).

The tradition has continued in the Church to pray and anoint with oil in the Lord's name for the purpose of helping the sick and forgiving their sins. This is the origin of the Church's sacrament of the Anointing of the Sick. It is God's will that we should fight strenuously against all sickness and disease while we seek the blessings of good health, wholeness in body, mind and spirit. Besides having recourse to prayer for healing we should also use effective natural means for preserving and restoring health, encourage the care of the sick and seek through study, research and medicine to cure disease.

Prayer for healing can flow spontaneously, directly from our heart, crying out to God to heal. It may simply occur in the strong, inner desire of our being as we desire the healing of the sick person with every fibre of our being as the most important need in our lives at the moment. Healing may flow as we enter into the presence of the Lord, prayerfully being aware that He is present, attentive, compassionate and active. Our prayer may be silent, expressed in words, groans, song or in the prayer language of the charism of tongues. Change or healing is not found in what we say but in what the Lord says. That means we must sensitively listen to what God may speak as He communicates His will to us. The charisms of word of knowledge, word of wisdom and faith may all be operative to bring about healing or miracle. The word of knowledge can be considered as God's diagnosis of the situation while the word of wisdom gives God's direction as to how to deal with the diagnosis. The charisms are manifestations of the Holy Spirit at work through our prayer giving enlightenment, understanding, wisdom, counsel or whatever is needed to bring healing, wholeness and holiness as God's response to the prayer offered.

Prayer may be needed to heal soul/spirit hurts, negative memories or wounds, so that the inner person may grow strong, overcome their weaknesses and walk freely in the light of Christ. The prayer of forgiveness is often so necessary when it comes to the need for healing, so that healing can take place. To forgive those who have harmed us or have burdened us with guilt or shame or made us feel insecure, inferior or inadequate is absolutely necessary. To forgive is a decision that must be made. To heal the wound is what God does. When it is difficult to forgive, we need to begin by simply asking for the desire to desire to forgive. We find healing when the forgiveness is given and we are able to pray for the one who has caused the pain that they be blessed just as we would want ourselves to be blessed in super-abundance by the Lord.

In praying for healing one may follow the practice of journalling, keeping a record of God's input through daily prayer. One may practice centering prayer by placing one's focus directly on the Lord, waiting on Him in silence while contemplating God's presence and using a particular prayer word if distractions come and you need to refocus. Praying with the Sacred Scriptures through meditating on a particular passage or by entering into a contemplative form of prayer by placing one's self through the faculty of the imagination into the scripture scene are other ways of entering prayer for healing. To heal addictions always involves or requires a decision of the will for freedom, and prayer to break the hold of the evil one on the person's life may be necessary.

The Bible is a handbook for healing. We don't read the Bible for God's benefit but for our own. The Bible helps us in our conversation with the Lord God, and He can inspire us through the Holy Spirit to read particular passages that speak to our individual or group need at that moment. The more familiar we are with the Sacred Scriptures the more our mind is renewed, our passion for Jesus is stirred up; the more we live and speak the truth, the more we are formed in God's image and likeness, His character, stance and outreach.

To be immersed or soaked in prayer brings about steady improvement in the sick. To be surrounded by loving people who trust and have faith, who turn to the Lord on behalf of the sick, praying regularly for a period of time each day or week can bring transformation to the mind, heart, spirit and body of the sick person whose faith and trust in the Lord is deepened.

Prayer for healing may be offered in any situation at any time to individuals or in large or small healing services. The prayer may be offered in various ways, but always there should be an encouragement to expectant faith so that the recipients of the prayer are open and receptive to what the Lord may do. The largest group in which I have prayed for healing occurred several years ago in India. The gathered crowd numbered approximately forty thousand people and I was given ten minutes to speak to the multitude gathered under thatched roofs. At the moment I opened my mouth to speak, heaven itself opened as the torrential rain poured down. Instantly we were an island in the middle of a lake. I simply said, "As God is pouring down His rain to water and bless the earth, so He is pouring down His healing and blessing upon all of us." Instantly, spontaneously, healing took place everywhere throughout the crowd. We had gathered together for a day of prayer, and with simple faith there was openness and receptivity for the Lord to heal His people.

Often in ministry the laying on of hands is offered to the sick. This is a scriptural tradition and communicates God's loving touch, healing, peace and freedom to those who receive it. It is a very natural way to minister and is found in homes and hospitals everywhere. The parent who holds, comforts, strokes a child who is crying or upset, the visitor who places a hand on the shoulder or holds hands with the sick one while desiring their healing, are ministering naturally with the laying on of hands. This gesture is used in many situations to empower, to bless, to comfort, to mission or to heal by passing on the grace of the Holy Spirit.

Blessed oil, used as a sacramental, is often used as one prays for healing, anointing the sick on the forehead and/or hands as the one who anoints offers prayer for healing. Oil, a sign of strength and an agent of healing, is used to be an external sign of the presence of the Holy Spirit ministering healing in the name of Jesus. Sometimes people use holy water, blessed water, blessed salt as support to their prayer ministry, expecting the Lord to act as they exercise their faith and pray to the Lord for healing. The people of God are very comfortable with the use of sacramentals as an aid to faith. But it is faith in Jesus that is all-important. He is the Healer. There is no other.

Healing is an ongoing process whereas a cure means that the difficulty has been completely dealt with. Healing is always necessary and comes in a variety of ways as a person is brought to wholeness. God intervenes directly to bring wholeness to the individual. Healing is God's work in the life of an individual. We know the prayer for healing is answered when the pain disappears, movement is restored, symptoms of illness disappear, the person knows peace; fear is gone; life, energy, vitality is restored and joy, wonder and awe at God's goodness is experienced.

A person may pray alone or with others for healing. A team of people may pray together with one leading the prayer and the others acting as support as they minister love and a healing touch. The one leading the prayer ministers the power of the Word of God, focusses the attention of those gathered and speaks with authority to invite the Lord's direct intervention to bring healing. It is in the climate of faith and expectancy that people are most free to receive the answer to prayer that the Lord provides.

Chapter 3

SCRIPTURAL FOUNDATIONS

The psalms of the Old Testament are the eternal prayers of the people of God, many of which are attributed to the authorship of David. They express the human condition both in the days of David and today. The psalms contain the wealth of human experience expressed in dependence on the Lord for deliverance and healing in times of need and in praise and thanksgiving to God in times of celebration, recognizing the sovereignty, majesty and goodness of the Almighty.

The psalmist cries, "Pity me, Yahweh, I have no strength left, heal me, my bones are in torment, my soul is in utter torment. Yahweh, how long will you be?" (Psalm 6:2-3). Trust and confidence in the Lord are expressed in the midst of desperate need. Another psalm speaks, "Yahweh, Restorer of Jerusalem! He brought back Israel's exiles, healing their broken hearts, and binding up their wounds" (Psalm 147:2-3). Our God is a healer, one who provides for His people in all circumstances.

Among the stories told in the Old Testament are several that speak of God healing barrenness in childless women: Sarah who gives birth to Isaac (Genesis 18:10-14), the wife of Manoah who became the mother of Samson (Judges 13:5, 24), Samuel's mother, Hannah (1 Samuel 1:19-20), and the Shunammite woman who was blessed by the prophet Elisha (2 Kings 4:16-17). All experienced the favour of the living God.

The prophets Elijah and Elisha – both mighty in speaking God's Word and in performing miracles – pray for healing and God answers their prayers. The Scripture tells of how they brought healing and restoration of life to the sons of the women who had befriended them (1 Kings 17:17-23;

2 Kings 4:18-37). Elisha's healing of Naaman the leper is also told and he comes to believe in the living God who heals (2 Kings 5:1-15).

The prophet Isaiah speaks of the coming of the Messiah and restoration and healing through Him ... the kingdom of peace and fulfilment would be ushered in. He speaks of the Messiah as the suffering servant of God:

> And yet ours were the sufferings he bore, ours the
> sorrows he carried. But we, we thought of him as
> someone punished, struck by God, and brought low.
> Yet he was pierced through for our faults, crushed for
> our sins. On him lies a punishment that brings us
> peace, and through his wounds we are healed
> (Isaiah 53:4-5).

The promise being fulfilled by the Lord God to save His people is revealed in the mission of the prophet. We read:

> The spirit of the Lord Yahweh has been given to me,
> for Yahweh has anointed me. He has sent me to bring
> good news to the poor, to bind up hearts that are
> broken; to proclaim liberty to captives, freedom to
> those in prison; to proclaim a year of favour from
> Yahweh ... to comfort all those who mourn ... for he
> has clothed me in the garments of salvation, he has
> wrapped me in the cloak of integrity (Isaiah 61:1-11).

As recorded in Luke's gospel, Jesus applies these words of Isaiah to Himself when He reads from the scroll of Isaiah in the synagogue of Nazareth at the beginning of His public ministry (cf. Luke 4:14-19). The ministry of Jesus included preaching, teaching, healing, exorcism and the formation of disciples who would carry on His ministry after Him. Signs and wonders, healings and miracles accompanied the proclamation that the kingdom of God had come near with Jesus in the midst of the people. All who embraced Jesus, followed Him, became His disciples, were empowered by the same Spirit that empowered Jesus in ministry. Jesus made real, tangible, available, the love and compassion of God the Father for His people. For Jesus, healing was essential in His ministry. It was part of proclaiming the Good News, an essential part, so that there was no doubt that God cared and was reaching out to intervene in the lives of all who heard the Good News of salvation, the Father's love revealed through His only-begotten Son become man in the flesh.

John the Baptist sent his disciples to Jesus to inquire whether He was "the one who is to come" (Luke 7:19) and Jesus points to what He is doing as answer to their question:

> It was just then that he cured many people of diseases and afflictions and of evil spirits, and gave the gift of sight to many who were blind. Then he gave the messengers their answer, "Go back and tell John what you have seen and heard: the blind see again, the lame walk, lepers are cleansed, and the deaf hear, the dead are raised to life, the Good News is proclaimed to the poor and happy is the man who does not lose faith in me" (Luke 7:22-23).

Healing, for Jesus, is a sign that God's kingdom is already being revealed, the promises of the Old Testament are being realized before their eyes and in their hearing. While the Church focuses more on the teaching of Jesus, it was primarily as a healer that the gospels focus on Jesus and His ministry. Jesus is the Man of the Spirit having received the Spirit "without measure" (John 3:34). It is in the power of the Spirit that His signs, His works, His wonders are performed as He calls forth faith, expectant faith, in the lives of those who receive His ministry. So often Jesus says to a person, "Your faith has made you well." Yet Jesus lived in a time, not unlike our own, that was characterized by unbelief but "the Power of the Lord was behind his works of healing" (Luke 5:17). For Jesus, faith and prayer were essential as evidenced by His commendations of faith and His frequent recourse to prayer for extended periods of time. Jesus told the woman who touched the hem of His garment in order to obtain healing, "Your faith has restored you to health; go in peace and be free

21

of your complaint" (Mark 5:34).

The Power of the Spirit was in Jesus and He knew when "that power had gone out from him" (Mark 5:30). In the parables told by Jesus we see the wonderful, compassionate love of the Father, the need to forgive and the willingness to minister to those who have been wounded or weakened in the course of their daily lives. By the light of the Spirit we are to seek God's wisdom and the grace to meet the needs of others as we bring God's compassionate love into practical action.

In the gospels we see Jesus responding to the needs for which family members or friends interceded because they had the faith to come to Jesus knowing that if they did, Jesus would heal. At times it is persistence that pays off, bringing increased faith and healing. Jesus' healings are a sign to an unbelieving world, a faithless generation. The healings were for a purpose: to bring wholeness and holiness into the person's life. Jesus sought to call forth faith, to strengthen faith, to bring about real spiritual growth, a radical response so that those healed would follow Him on the Christian way, the journey through life to the heavenly kingdom. The Scriptures, though, do not indicate that all who were healed benefited spiritually or followed Jesus on "the way."

The gospels record in summary fashion that Jesus heals many although many individual accounts of healing are narrated. A typical day in the life of Jesus is recounted in Mark 1:16-34 in which Jesus calls His first four disciples, teaches in Capernaum, cures a demoniac, cures Simon's mother-in-law of fever, eats in Simon and Andrew's home, and then He cured many who were suffering from diseases of one kind or another. As recorded in Matthew 8:1-17, Jesus cures a leper, then the centurion's servant, then Peter's mother-in-law, then after eating, Jesus "cured all who were sick." Matthew concludes, "This was to fulfill the prophecy of Isaiah: He took our sicknesses away and carried our diseases for us." Jesus could take away bodily ills because His own suffering was expiatory and He could wipe away the effects, the consequence and the penalty of sin.

The miraculous healings of Jesus reveal His power over nature, sickness, death and the devil. Jesus calms the storm (Matthew 8:23-27) and walks on water (Matthew 14:22-33), astounding His disciples who wonder, "Whatever kind of man is this? Even the winds and the sea obey him" and they bow down before Him and say, "Truly, you are the Son of God." He raises the young daughter of an official to life (cf. Matthew 9:23-26). He restores to life the only son of the widow of Naim (cf. Luke 7:11-17). He raises Lazarus to life after four days in the tomb (cf. John 11:1-44). He casts out devils as in the case of the demoniacs of Gadara (cf. Matthew 8:28-34). The miracles Jesus worked are unique because of the spiritual and symbolic significance He attaches to them. His miracles declare that the messianic era has begun and blessings are being poured out on all who receive the Good News being proclaimed. They are the first signs of the Spirit's triumph over the empire of Satan and over all the powers of evil, whether of sin or disease. While compassion is often the motive for the miraculous healing of Jesus, the basic purpose is to strengthen faith.

When Jesus sent out His apostles to preach the kingdom, He gave them His own healing power. "He summoned his twelve disciples, and gave them authority over unclean spirits with power to cast them out and to cure all kinds of diseases and sickness" (Matthew 10:1). "Cure the sick, raise the dead, cleanse the lepers, cast out devils" (Matthew 10:8). Matthew, before giving the missionary discourse of chapter ten, recounts ten miracles performed by Jesus (cf. Matthew 8 and 9) as signs accrediting the missionary. Mark 16:17-18 records the signs that will be associated with believers, that will accompany them as they live and express their faith: "In my name they will cast out devils; they will have the gift of tongues; they will pick up snakes in their hands, and be unharmed should they drink deadly poison; they will lay their hands on the sick, who will recover."

The faith that Jesus asks for from the beginning of His public ministry is an act of trust and self-abandonment in which they no longer rely on their own strength but commit themselves to the power and guidance of the Spirit of Christ Jesus. This kind of faith is only lived in relationship with Christ Jesus. Jesus wants this kind of faith when He works His miracles which attest to His mission and witness to the kingdom. Without this kind of faith the miracles lose their true meaning. Mark 6:4-6 tells us that in Nazareth, His home town, Jesus "could work no miracle there, though he cured a few sick people by laying his hands on them. He was amazed at their lack of faith." Since faith requires a complete response of the whole person in mind and heart, it is not an easy act of humility for a person to perform and many are half-hearted when it comes to a faith response to Jesus. When faith is strong it works wonders as when a tiny seed of faith as big as a mustard seed can move a mountain (cf. Matthew 17:20). Jesus says, "If you have faith, everything you ask for in prayer you will receive" (Matthew 21:22). Jesus never refuses faith, especially when it asks for forgiveness of sin. "Courage, my child, your sins are forgiven," (Matthew 9:2) Jesus says to the paralytic. Faith is absolutely necessary for salvation, for healing. "It is the name of Jesus which, through our faith in it, has brought back the strength of this man whom you see here and who is well known to you. It is faith in that name that has restored this man to health, as you can all see" (Acts 3:26). Such were the words of Peter after the cure of the lame man at the Beautiful Gate.

Healing requires faith in God. Jesus is not just a miracle worker. Rather, it is faith in the power of God that is present in Jesus that calls for the healings needed by those who turn to Jesus in their need. The healings and exorcisms of Jesus are evidence, signs, that call for a decision to believe in the person of Jesus, the Son of God, in His message and in the "works" He does. The work of healing is the taking back, the breaking of the hold that evil has on the world. It is liberating people from the control of Satan who seeks to enslave and destroy. Healing is a sign that God is at work bringing about the salvation of the whole person – body, mind and spirit. Healing is such a precious gift of God eagerly sought after by those who believe that God heals and sets free. The Lord Jesus gives eternal life and this begins as a person places faith, trust and abandonment, in relationship with Jesus. As a person begins to live more and more under the lordship of Jesus Christ, wholeness and holiness develop more and more in the person as they begin to live for eternal life with Jesus who bestows healing and peace in the here and now.

Stories abound of the healing action of Jesus in countries of the Third World. Fewer stories are told in the more prosperous nations because of the lack of faith, complacency or unwillingness to change or to grow in relationship with Christ. Faith and expectation of God's action are so necessary. The ministry of Jesus focussed on preaching the kingdom and making disciples. When Jesus leaves Capernaum and travels throughout Galilee He says to His disciples, "'Let us go elsewhere, to the neighbouring country towns, so that I can preach there, too, because that is why I came.' And he went all through Galilee, preaching in their synagogues and casting out devils" (Mark 1:38-39). Jesus teaches the necessity of faith and the importance of prayer as a priority in one's life. He helps people grow in faith and He confronts the prevailing climate of unbelief. He saw His own ministry of healing and deliverance as evidence that He is the Messiah. "God had anointed him with the Holy Spirit and with power, and because God was with him, Jesus went about doing good and curing all who had fallen into the power of the devil" (Acts 10:38).

Healing is wholeness of the total person and his

environment. Healing is deliverance from demonic power and influence. Healing is forgiveness of sin. Forgiveness is a gift and with it comes the goodness of God which makes us acceptable. "For our sake God made the sinless one into sin, so that in him we might become the goodness of God" (1 Corinthians 5:21). This brings release and healing into all dimensions of life that have been affected by sin: the spirit, conscience, emotions, body, relationships and the circumstances of life. God's desire for us is that we live in good health, soundness of body, mind and spirit, by staying free from sin, guilt, condemnation, unforgiveness, hate, resentment and all that is negative and destructive (cf. Romans 8:1, 31-34). Healing is restoration from sickness, life from death, reigning victoriously in life through Christ Jesus. The process of healing in the Kingdom of God is total restoration, not only out of sickness but into God's reign right now. "If it is certain that death reigned over everyone as the consequence of one man's fall, it is even more certain that one man, Jesus Christ, will cause everyone to reign in life who receives the free gift that he does not deserve, of being made righteous" (Romans 5:17).

In the Acts of the Apostles we see the same Spirit of Jesus empowering the disciples for ministry. Peter and John at the Beautiful Gate in Jerusalem effect the cure of a lame man who was a cripple from birth. At the command of Peter, "In the name of Jesus Christ the Nazarene, walk!" he immediately receives complete healing and accompanies Peter and John into the Temple "walking and jumping and praising God" (cf. Acts 3:1-10). In Lydda, Peter effects the cure of a crippled man, Aeneas, a paralytic who had been bedridden for eight years, by commanding, "Aeneas, Jesus Christ cures you: get up and fold up your sleeping mat" (cf. Acts 9:32-35). At Jaffa, Peter raises a dead woman to life by saying to her "Tabitha, stand up" (cf. Acts 9:36-42). Acts 5:12a, 15, 16 tells us:

So many signs and wonders were worked among the

people at the hands of the apostles that the sick were taken out into the streets and laid on beds and sleeping-mats in the hope that at least the shadow of Peter might fall across some of them as he went past. People even came crowding in from the towns round about Jerusalem, bringing with them their sick and those tormented by unclean spirits, and all of them were cured.

Paul recognized that a man in the crowd to whom he was preaching had "the faith to be healed." Paul speaks out to him, "Get to your feet – stand up" and the cripple is immediately cured (cf. Acts 14:8-10). At Troas, Paul raises a dead man, Eutychus, to life after he had fallen three floors to his death (cf. Acts 20:7-12). Acts records how Paul, on the island of Malta, laid hands on the sick and they were healed (cf. Acts 28:8-10). The power of God was with his disciples who carried on His mission. "So remarkable were the miracles worked by God at Paul's hands that handkerchiefs or aprons which had touched him were taken to the sick, and they were cured of their illnesses, and the evil spirits came out of them" (Acts 19:11-12).

Philip proclaims Christ to a Samaritan town and the people welcome the message Philip preaches "because they had heard of the miracles he worked or because they saw them for themselves. There were, for example, unclean spirits that came shrieking out of many who were possessed, and several paralytics and cripples were cured" (cf. Acts 8:4-8).

Ananias "laid his hands on Saul and said, 'Brother Saul, I have been sent by the Lord Jesus who appeared to you on the way here so that you may recover your sight and be filled with the Holy Spirit.' Immediately it was as though scales fell away from Saul's eyes and he could see again" (Acts 9:17-18). Conversion takes place – transformation of heart – and Saul becomes Paul, mighty man of God, proclaiming Jesus Christ to the Gentiles.

Jesus is the Healer. In His name healing, cures, deliverance, exorcism are performed. The pages of Scripture are alive with Jesus who heals and sets free. The work of the Spirit continues to inflame the hearts of those who accept Jesus Christ as their only Lord and Saviour, their only Healer and Deliverer. Jesus is alive, risen from the dead, reigning in glory, ministering effectively through the presence, power and action of the Holy Spirit to those who will receive "new life" in His name.

The Church continues the mission of Jesus guided, empowered, led by the Holy Spirit. Countless disciples throughout the centuries minister in the name of Jesus Christ, continuing His healing ministry.

Chapter 4

HEALING THROUGH THE CENTURIES

The healing ministry of Jesus, at His command, was carried on by His disciples. Signs and wonders accompanied their ministry with astounding results. "The many miracles and signs worked through the apostles made a deep impression on everyone" (Acts 2:43) and the result was that, "Day by day the Lord added to their community those destined to be saved" (Acts 2:47). Joy, the sequel to faith, filled the believers who became part of the first community of faith in Jerusalem. "The apostles continued to testify to the resurrection of the Lord Jesus with great power" (Acts 4:33), and great generosity among those who believed was the result of putting their faith and trust in the Lord Jesus.

When active persecution began with the stoning of the deacon Stephen, many of the disciples went from place to place preaching the Good News of Jesus Christ. Philip, another deacon, preached to the Samaritans proclaiming the Christ to them.

> The people united in welcoming the message Philip preached, either because they had heard of the miracles he worked or because they saw them for themselves. There were, for example, unclean spirits that came shrieking out of many who were possessed, and several paralytics and cripples were cured. As a result, there was great rejoicing in that town (Acts 8:6-8).

The Church, as a result of the miracles, healings and exorcisms, grew rapidly wherever the disciples proclaimed the Good News of the Kingdom of God, that Jesus, the Son of God, had come, sent by God, as the Messiah who had been prophesied in the Old Testament. The works accomplished at the hands of His disciples were proof of the truth of the message that Jesus had risen from the dead and was with them in the power of the Holy Spirit. Jesus, risen, was very much alive!

The Church was established in many places, wherever the disciples travelled proclaiming Jesus Christ. "The Lord helped them, and a great number believed and were converted to the Lord" (Acts 11:21). Barnabas, "a good man, filled with the Holy Spirit and with faith" (Acts 11:24) travelled to Antioch to encourage the Greek converts with the result that many people came to believe in Christ Jesus and were added to the faith. The hand of the Lord was with His Church. "So remarkable were the miracles worked by God at Paul's hands that handkerchiefs or aprons which had touched him were taken to the sick, and they were cured of their illnesses, and the evil spirits came out of them" (Acts 19:11).

> So many signs and wonders were worked among the people at the hands of the apostles that the sick were even taken out into the streets and laid on beds and sleeping-mats in the hope that at least the shadow of Peter might fall across some of them as he went past. People even came crowding in from the towns round about Jerusalem, bringing with them their sick and those tormented by unclean spirits, and all of them were cured" (Acts 5:15-16).

As the people witnessed healings and miracles take place, more were healed. Faith was stirred up and great expectation of healing and freedom was produced in those who were attracted to the message proclaimed and the mighty deeds of power being worked in the name of Jesus.

The disciples of Jesus learned to do what He did. They learned to do the Father's works. With the power of the Spirit infilling them they proclaimed the reign of God, and by the same Spirit working signs and wonders through them the Church started at Pentecost grew rapidly. In every town, culture and race, among the Jews and Gentiles the work of proclamation was accompanied by mighty signs as the sick were healed, the possessed freed and the faith was rooted in the hearts of those who came to believe. Jesus had sent out His disciples with authority and power "to proclaim the kingdom of God and to heal" (Luke 9:2). As they began to exercise that authority and power, they received more. As they witnessed demons cast out and the sick healed of their infirmities and sicknesses, their faith strengthened. They knew the Lord was with them, and led by the Holy Spirit they expected and called forth signs and wonders. When Jesus sent out the twelve and then the seventy-two disciples, He multiplied His own ministry, expanding the kingdom of God. The greater the number of Christians performing signs and wonders, the greater the impact on the culture and the times, on the hearts and lives of the people. The disciples "going out preached everywhere, the Lord working with them and confirming the word by the signs that accompanied it" (Mark 16:20). Signs and wonders, miracles, healings and exorcisms were a part of the daily life of the early Christians. They expected these to happen. It was normal Christianity for the disciples of Jesus.

Unfortunately, over the centuries various opinions have been held about the continuance or non-continuance of the miracle ministry of Jesus and the disciples. Some hold that the signs and wonders ceased at the end of the apostolic age, about the end of the first century; signs and wonders were God's way of getting the Church started. Once the Church was established there was no longer a need for "signs" to validate the proclamation of the gospel. Some hold that the signs and wonders ceased as faith for miracles disappeared because a mature faith based on reason and enlightenment does not need such signs and wonders. But, in reality, signs and wonders have never ceased though through the centuries they occur in varying degrees. The history of the Church bears witness to the reality.

Quadratus who wrote about 125 A.D. knew people who

had been healed by Jesus and he gives witness to the effects of the healing ministry of Jesus:

> But the works of our Saviour were always present, for they were true, those who were cured, those who rose from the dead, who not merely appeared as cured and risen, but were constantly present, not only while the Saviour was living, but even for some time after he had gone, so that some of them survived even to our own time.[1]

Justin Martyr (ca. 100-165) was a Christian apologist and wrote in his *Second Apology* (ca. 153) concerning exorcism and healing:

> For numberless demoniacs throughout the whole world, and in your city, many of our Christian men exorcising them in the name of Jesus Christ, who was crucified under Pontius Pilate, have healed and do heal, rendering helpless and driving the possessing devils out of the men, though they could not be cured by all the other exorcists, and those who used incantations and drugs.[2]

Irenaeus (140-203), the bishop of Lyons, was a theologian and pastor who wrote five books against the heresy of Gnosticism. In writing he testifies:

> Those who are in truth Christ's disciples, receiving grace from him, do in his name perform miracles.... For some do certainly and truly drive out devils, so that those who have been cleansed from evil spirits frequently join themselves to the Church.... Others still, heal the sick by laying their hands upon them, and they are made whole. Yea, moreover, as I have said, the dead even have been raised up, and remained among us for many years. And what shall I more say? It is not possible to name the number of gifts which the Church, throughout the whole world, has received from God, in the name of Jesus Christ.[3]

Tertullian (ca. 160-220) was a prolific writer and in his work *To Scapula*, chapter 5, he gives an account of expelling demons and healing:

> The clerk of one of them who was liable to be thrown upon the ground by an evil spirit was set free from his affliction, and was also the relative of another, and the little boy of a third. How many men of rank (to say nothing of common people) have been delivered from devils, and healed of diseases! Even Severus himself, the father of Antonine, was graciously mindful of the Christians; for he sought out the Christian Proculus, surnamed Torpacion, the steward of Euhodias, and in gratitude for his having once cured him by anointing, he kept him in his palace till the day of his death.[4]

Novatian (210-280) of Rome, in Chapter 29 of *Treatise Concerning the Trinity*, writes of the Holy Spirit:

> This is He who places prophets in the Church, instructs teachers, directs tongues, gives powers and healings, does wonderful works, offers discrimination of spirits, affords powers of government, suggests counsels, and orders and arranges whatever other gifts there are of charismata; and thus make the Lord's Church everywhere, and in all, perfected and completed.[5]

Origen (c. 185-254) witnesses to the power of exorcism and healing in the name of Jesus:

> Some display evidence of having received some miraculous power because of this faith (in Jesus), shown in the people they cure, upon those who need healing they use no other invocation than that of the supreme God and of the name of Jesus, together with the history about him. By these also we have seen many delivered from serious ailments, and from natural distractions and madness, and countless other diseases, which neither men nor demons had cured.[6]

The *Apostolic Constitutions* give a summary of the testimony of the early Church Fathers and point to the primary purpose of the signs that accompanied the proclamation of the Good News: so that the Kingdom of God would be established on earth and that people would come to believe.

> These gifts were first bestowed upon us, the apostles, when we were about to preach the Gospel to every creature, and afterwards it was necessarily provided to those who had now come to faith through our agency, not for the advantage of those who performed them, but for the conviction of unbelievers, that those whom the word did not persuade, the power of signs might put to shame.[7]

Augustine (354-430) was bishop of Hippo, and near the end of his life he wrote *The City of God* (ca. 413-427) in which he details the miracles that were occurring in his city. In Chapter 28, Book 22, Augustine writes:

> It is sometimes objected that the miracles, which Christians claimed to have occurred, no longer happen... The truth is that even today miracles are being wrought in the name of Christ, sometimes through His sacraments and sometimes through the intercession of the relics of the saints.... It is a simple fact that there is no lack of miracles even in our day. And the God who works the miracles we read of in the scriptures uses any means and manner he chooses.

The lives of the saints down through the ages tell of wonderful miracles, works of healing and exorcism, revealing the ministry of the Holy Spirit in the name of Jesus. St. Martin of Tours (336-397), St. Francis of Assisi (1181-1226), St. Vincent Ferrer (1350-1419), St. Vincent dePaul (1580-1660), St. Jean Marie Vianney, the Curé d'Ars (1786-1859), and countless other saints have been recognized throughout the centuries for the power of Jesus at work in and through them. The process of beatification and canonization by the Roman Catholic Church requires proof of miracle and healing worked through the intercession of the deceased "holy ones." Pope John Paul II, during his pontificate, beatified or canonized more people than has been done in the whole course of the life of the Church.

St. Philip Neri (b. 1515), the founder of the Oratorians, had a major healing ministry. He prayed for healing with the laying on of hands while he fostered expectant faith in the recipients of his prayer. The Lord Jesus worked through him to minister healing. As people placed faith and trust that God would work through him to heal, they received the reward of faith and answer to their prayers.

The ministry of healing has never ceased in the Church and it is especially present in the poor and the sick who reach out in faith to Jesus for healing and wholeness. While some theologians, scholars and writers discourage people from expecting miracle or healing to happen, experience is that they occur every day. Where people pray for healing, expecting much, expecting the Lord to minister, healing does take place. Today, we witness healing and miracles as a regular occurrence in the ministry of evangelists, in major healing crusades, as we do at shrines of Mary and the saints. People experience renewed faith, peace, oneness with the Lord, even miracles and healing, as they place faith in the Lord and His will to heal. Many place faith in special prayers, devotions, relics and novenas, trusting the Lord to answer.

Today, following the Second Vatican Council (1962-1965), there is a much greater awareness of the Holy Spirit and empowerment by the Spirit of Jesus to minister healing. Especially through the Charismatic Renewal the ministry of healing is being restored to the Church as people enter into an abiding personal relationship with Jesus Christ in the power of the Spirit. Men, women and children, the ordained and the unordained, are exercising their expectant faith and are ministering healing by the power of the Spirit. As people commit their lives under the lordship of Jesus Christ, their eyes are opened to the truth of the Gospel and they receive the empowerment of the Spirit to continue the mission of Jesus, the work of the Spirit, to renew all of creation. The gifts of the Spirit are a vital part of this ministry and outreach.

Chapter 5

SACRAMENTS OF HEALING

While all the sacraments can be the vehicle for the Lord's healing to occur, two in particular are the way in which the Church continues the healing ministry of Jesus Christ: the sacrament of Anointing the Sick and the sacrament of Penance. The Lord Jesus Christ, the Great Physician, wills that His Church continue to bring healing and salvation in the power of the Holy Spirit to the members of the Church, the People of God. When Jesus healed the paralytic, forgiving his sins and restoring him to physical health, He said: "Which is easier to say, 'Your sins are forgiven' or to say, 'Get up, pick up your stretcher and walk'?" (Mark 2:9). Jesus both forgives and heals.

SACRAMENT OF ANOINTING OF THE SICK

By the sacred anointing of the sick and the prayer of the priests, the whole Church commends those who are ill to the suffering and glorified Lord, that he may raise them up and save them. And indeed she exhorts them to contribute to the good of the People of God by freely uniting themselves to the Passion and death of Christ.[8]

Illness and suffering can be part of every human life, sometimes producing fear, despair, anxiety, anger at God or they can lead a person closer to God as the focus shifts to what is really important in life.

In Old Testament times, illness was seen to be the result of sin, evil, and by conversion, turning from sin towards the living God, one could be restored, renewed, healed. God is faithful and He says, "It is I, Yahweh, who gives you healing" (Exodus 15:26). The prophet Isaiah in speaking of the future

37

for God's people says, "No one living there shall say, 'I am sickly'; the people who live there will be forgiven all their faults" (Isaiah 33:24).

The Gospels witness to the compassionate love of Jesus that responded to the sick and their many kinds of illness and infirmity. Jesus heals and forgives, reaching out to bring wholeness to body, mind and spirit. The power to heal resides in and flows from Him as He is moved by the Holy Spirit and fulfills the will of His heavenly Father. Jesus even identified Himself with the sick: "I was ... sick and you visited me" (Matthew 25:36). Jesus continues to love the sick and to reach out to them in their need through the sacraments.

Jesus placed great emphasis on having faith. He told the woman with a longstanding haemorrhage, "Your faith has restored you to health; go in peace and be free from your complaint" (Mark 5:34). He tells Jairus, the father of a young girl who has died, "Only have faith" (Mark 5:37), and He raises the girl to life. Jesus healed in different ways, using signs to minister healing, such as the laying on of hands, spittle, mud, washing. He simply spoke a word or gave a touch, a command, and healing took place. Power went out from Him. "All those who touched him were cured" (Mark 6:56).

> The Holy Spirit gives to some a special charism of healing so as to make manifest the power of the grace of the risen Lord. But even the most intense prayers do not always obtain the healing of all illnesses. Thus St. Paul must learn from the Lord that "my grace is sufficient for you, for my power is made perfect in weakness" and that the sufferings to be endured can mean that "in my flesh I complete what is lacking in Christ's afflictions for the sake of his Body, that is, the Church."[9]

The Church has been commanded by the Lord to "heal the sick!" (Matthew 10:8). The Church down through the centuries has tried to be faithful to the Lord's command by caring for the sick personally or through establishing hospitals, hospices, treatment centres that reach out to minister the compassionate, loving care of Jesus for the sick. Intercessory prayer for the sick is commonly exercised by all the faithful. The Church

> [...] believes in the life-giving presence of Christ, the physician of souls and bodies. This presence is particularly active through the sacraments, and in an altogether special way through the Eucharist, the bread that gives eternal life and that St. Paul suggests is connected with bodily health.[10]

The early apostolic Church had established a particular way of ministering to the sick.

> If one of you is ill, he should send for the elders of the Church, and they must anoint him with oil in the name of the Lord and pray over him. The prayer of faith will save the sick man and the Lord will raise him up again; and if he has committed any sins, he will be forgiven (James 5:14-15). By the Church this has been recognized as one of the seven sacraments, encounters with the risen Lord, Jesus Christ.[11]

> This sacred anointing of the sick was instituted by Christ our Lord as a true and proper sacrament of the New Testament. It is alluded to indeed by Mark, but is recommended to the faithful and promulgated by James the apostle and brother of the Lord.[12]

> From ancient times in the liturgical traditions of both East and West, we have testified to the practice of anointings of the sick with blessed oil. Over the centuries the Anointing of the Sick was conferred more and more exclusively on those at the point of death. Because of this it received the name "Extreme Unction." Notwithstanding this evolution the liturgy has never failed to beg the Lord that the sick person may recover his health if it would be conducive to his salvation.[13]

Pope Paul VI, after the Second Vatican Council, published an *Apostolic Constitution* in which he set forth in the

Roman Rite:

> The sacrament of Anointing of the Sick is given to
> those who are seriously ill by anointing them on the
> forehead and hands with duly blessed oil – pressed
> from olives or from other plants – saying only once:
> "Through this holy anointing may the Lord in his love
> and mercy help you with the grace of the Holy Spirit.
> May the Lord who frees you from sin save you and
> raise you up."[14]

The Anointing of the Sick should be administered
whenever anyone begins to be in danger of death from
sickness or from old age. It should not be reserved only for
those who are at the point of leaving this life. The sacrament
can certainly be repeated if the health condition becomes
more serious. It should even be administered by the priest
before serious surgery. The one who receives the sacrament
should, if possible, be prepared to receive the sacrament with
the right dispositions, at least by intending to receive what the
Church offers through the sacrament. The sacrament is
conferred by the priest in prayer as his hands are silently laid
on the sick and then the anointing with blessed oil takes place.

The sacrament confers the grace of the Holy Spirit
which strengthens the recipient and imparts peace and courage
to overcome temptation and anxiety. Trust and faith in the
Lord is renewed and deepened, healing of soul and spirit takes
place and physical healing may occur. The recipient's sins are
forgiven as they are open to receive the life of grace. The sick
may experience a real union with the passion and suffering of
Christ giving witness to the love and saving work of Jesus, the
Christ.

For those departing this life the sacrament is a
preparation for the final journey as their sins are forgiven and
they are strengthened by the sacrament and receive the
Eucharist, food for the journey, the passing into eternal life.

The Anointing of the Sick completes our conformity to

the death and Resurrection of Christ, just as Baptism began it. It completes the holy anointings that mark the whole Christian life: that of Baptism which sealed the new life in us, and that of Confirmation which strengthened us for the combat of this life. This last anointing fortifies the end of our earthly life like a solid rampart for the final struggles before entering the Father's house.[15]

The Anointing of the Sick is a wonderful gift of the Lord Jesus to His Church for by it the sick person is united to the passion of Christ, for his own blessing and that of all the People of God. Strength, peace, courage help the Christian to give witness as to how one deals with the sufferings of sickness or old age. If the person has not been able to receive absolution of their sins through the sacrament of Reconciliation, then forgiveness of sins is effected by this sacrament. The sacrament is always effective restoring health, bringing wholeness to soul and spirit, and restoring bodily health if it is conducive to the person's salvation.

SACRAMENT OF PENANCE AND RECONCILIATION

The sacrament of Penance and Reconciliation is the sacrament of conversion, of confession and forgiveness, which makes sacramentally present the call of Jesus to real conversion of heart and life. For the baptized, who will experience the frailty and weakness of human nature and the inclination to sin, need all the help possible so that they have the victory in the struggle of living the Christian life. Conversion is an ongoing process as one strives for holiness on their journey towards eternal life.

Sin is a rejection of God's love, a self-destruction of one's own human dignity as a child of the living God, a stain upon the spiritual well-being, the holiness, of the Church. Sin weakens and destroys the grace-life received in Baptism. But it is God's grace, His mercy, that calls the sinner to repentance and transformation, to return to the intimate communion with God which was lost by sin. Conversion and repentance involves sorrow for sin committed and the firm decision to sin no more. Conversion seeks to make right the past and to establish the future in righteousness, holiness and goodness. This is achieved by placing one's hope in God's mercy, repenting of the wrongdoing, confessing one's sins to the priest in confession and having the intention to make reparation for the wrong done. True sorrow for sin flows from love of God that is stirred up in the heart of the penitent. It is only the priest, who has received the faculty of absolving from the authority of the Church, who can forgive sins in the name of Jesus Christ.

The spiritual effects of the sacrament of Reconciliation include the restoration to intimate communion with God in the life of grace, being reconciled with the Church, the remission of the eternal punishment incurred by mortal sin and the temporal punishment which results from sin. An increase of spiritual strength, peace and spiritual consolation, serenity of conscience, joy and healing result.

Everyone is faced with the reality of sin all around us and in our own lives. Everyone needs to know freedom and peace. Stress abounds in the world today and many are given to selfishness, pride, rebellion, stubbornness. Indeed, many live without hope.

Sin is a wound in a person's inner most self. We are all affected by the original sin of our first parents. When they were sent out of the garden, they weren't told to send their children back in, but they were told that a messiah would come. Each of us has our own original sin when we first turn against God's will. We each embrace personal sin when we abuse our own freedom. Every sin is personal but at the same time every sin is social; what we do affects others; what we do changes us so that we become more self-centred and less loving toward others. Every person has responsibility toward others, self and even to God.

God has called us to be holy, to know who He is, His holiness, to know the holiness of others and to know our own holiness. There is a growth process in the spiritual life whereby we recognize that sin is sin. No matter whether it is mortal or venial, serious or simple imperfections, we are to root out sin. Ideally, we would never extinguish the light of Christ in us or stain our baptismal robe with sin, but the reality is that we do. We see in baptism our conversion, our reconciliation with God and the Christian faith community. When baptismal innocence is lost, we have the sacrament of Reconciliation to make us clean again, to purify our hearts and intentions so that we may continue on as the disciples of Jesus.

How do I know I need to be reconciled? How do I know what my sins are? We could ask the Holy Spirit to reveal them to us or we could ask those we live with what they are. To know when to be reconciled we need to check the signs of slippage that may be evident in our lives. Such signs are foul language; (usually don't); being grumpy, angry, easily aroused to anger; don't enjoy going to Mass or reading scripture (it can taste dry – like sand or sawdust); being impatient; being selfish; not loving , not feeling like helping others; the conscience stops bothering, no awareness of sin (I'm not so bad, I'm OK); don't feel like eating, sleeping. If any of these signs are present in your life, you need to be reconciled.

All of us need a profound transformation of our hearts through the re-discovery of the Father's mercy and through victory over misunderstanding and hostility among brothers and sisters. We gain conversion of heart and victory over sin by faithful and loving attention to God's word, through personal and community prayer and through the sacraments, especially Reconciliation, although the reconciling grace of Jesus Christ is available in all the sacraments. Preaching, pastoral action and witness are the other means by which

Reconciliation can take place.

In 1 John 1:8-9 we are told: "If we say we have no sin, we deceive ourselves, and the truth is not in us. If we confess our sins, He is faithful and just and will forgive our sins." Contrition is the beginning and heart of conversion. Contrition is a clear and decisive rejection of sin committed together with the resolution not to commit it again, out of the love one has for God and which is reborn with repentance. Contrition and conversion are even more a drawing near to the holiness of God. It is a rediscovery of one's true identify which has been disturbed by sin. It is a liberation in the very depth of self, a regaining of lost joy, the joy of being saved by Jesus.

Nothing is more personal and intimate than this sacrament in which the sinner stands alone before God with his sin, repentance and trust in the mercy of God. In the process of conversion we turn away from serious sin, then venial sin, and then we work to correct our faults, our failings, our imperfections because even these hinder a true reflection of Jesus Christ through us. We may struggle with our "daily sins," with our humanity, with the whole idea of confessing and admitting "my sin" to another. But if we want to be healed and set free we need to humble ourselves and take the step that leads to freedom: confession, turning away from sin, choosing the path of holiness, goodness, righteousness. By approaching to receive the welcome back "hug of Christ" we blossom anew in God's love, His peace and joy.

The power to live as disciples of Jesus, in relationship with Jesus, comes as we yield to the move of the Holy Spirit in our lives. It is through the action of the Spirit that we receive the grace of conversion of heart, that we are empowered to walk as disciples of Jesus. Intimacy between the disciple's heart and Jesus' heart is most necessary. The Holy Spirit is given by Jesus to transform and equip disciples to do what He wants us to do. We all need the touch of the Master, fine-tuning us, so that we may resonate with the love of God.

Through receiving forgiveness we receive healing of our inner person, our spirit, our mind, emotions, even our body. But we must also forgive; just as we receive God's forgiveness, we must forgive: God, self and others. When we receive reconciliation, God remembers our sin no more – it is over and gone. It sometimes seems more difficult to forgive ourselves, but in the name of Jesus it can be done. To offer reconciliation to another, to forgive so that we can be forgiven is the way to healing, wholeness, sanctity. Through the sacrament of Reconciliation the confessor may pray for inner healing, deliverance, healing of memories, emotions, body. To be healed we must give the Lord permission not only to "clean house" but to set us free and to stir up the grace life within us. To be healed and free we must recognize that God is God and I am not; we must decide to follow Him faithfully.

A saint is a very human person in whom Jesus lives again. The love of God and the love of others are indissolubly connected. The only way to prove we love God is to love those whom God loves. The only way to prove that God is within our hearts is constantly to show the love of others within our lives. When we walk with the Lord Jesus, in intimate relationship with Him, not ahead of Him or behind Him or off to the side, we walk with a pure heart, a clean heart. We give up all sin for Him, for more of Him. Confession anyone? Go and be healed, made new, made whole.

SACRAMENT OF THE EUCHARIST

In every Mass we pray, "... only say the word and I shall be healed." In the Scriptures we are frequently told about the miracles and healings, the signs and the works of Jesus and His disciples. We are encouraged to have "expectant faith" that the same Jesus is continually ministering to us through the power and action of the Holy Spirit as hearts are touched, lives are renewed and transformed, people are given hope, courage and encouragement as needs are met, prayers are answered and faith comes alive.

We are called into a covenant relationship with our God where He is our God and we are His people. This is a relationship of pure intimacy wherein we meet our beloved and He gazes at us with love. We look at Him and He looks at us. We receive Him, body and blood, soul and divinity, whole and entire when we receive communion, the living risen Lord, so that we may be one with Him and with the whole mystical Body of Christ. This intimate reception of Jesus is both personal and communal. There is no such thing as private worship at Mass. We are always part of the Body, part of the communion of Saints, at the eucharistic celebration with all the angels and saints as we offer worship, praise, thanksgiving to our heavenly Father together with Jesus in the power of the Spirit.

The early Christians recognized the risen Lord in their midst as they ate the Lord's Supper just as the apostles recognized Him in the upper room as they ate fish together. The Eucharist looked back to the Last Supper meal and ahead to the heavenly banquet of the New Jerusalem. But in the present they expected to see the risen Lord revealed in their midst. That is why they prayed the "Marantha" – come, Lord Jesus. It was not just an invocation for the Lord's second coming at the end of time but an invitation for the Lord to come NOW in this particular Eucharist. The expectation was for Jesus to stretch out His hand, to work His signs and wonders.

In Eucharist we receive Jesus but He must receive us. His great love is revealed to us as we celebrate, making present again the sacrifice of His body and blood, according to the order of Melchizedek, in the bread and wine offered to the Father by the power of the Spirit. We receive the sacrifice back as our spiritual food and nourishment in the communion once the Father has accepted it. He always accepts the gift of His Son that is always pleasing to Him.

Intimacy with God is the kiss of God's presence wherein the heart of God is revealed, where we receive a foretaste of glory, a glimpse of the heavenly ecstasy. We are kissed by the love of God. We enter the secret place of the Most High, His presence, and drink deeply from the wellspring of His salvation. As the deer longs for the water so we long for the Lord. We pour out our hearts to Him, give Him first place, develop a sensitivity to His presence, His mystery. We yield to the God of surprises, give Him control, press deeply into His presence. We offer Him real, genuine, vulnerable, heart-felt, persistent prayer. We approach Him with an expectant heart, overwhelmed by His presence. He is our Beloved, Life itself, the Baptizer, the Healer, the wholly desirable one, the heavenly Bridegroom, Jesus.

Intimacy is a relationship with another that flows from a depth of knowledge and understanding that is shared by no one but the two individuals. It requires making choices and taking risks. It involves disclosure, revealing the real you, your innermost self, your hidden thoughts, feelings, emotions, needs. It requires honesty, transparency before the Lord. Who is your Beloved? The one who invites you to discover a depth of relationship you never dreamed existed. It is secure, settled, secret. It is that place of relationship, knowledge and love of Jesus, Jesus who heals, sets free, makes new.

More and more people are approaching Jesus in adoration of the Blessed Sacrament during exposition finding peace, intimacy, transformation, healing, just being in His presence. Everywhere, people are going to Jesus at what are called "Healing Masses" or Masses with prayer for healing. There is expectancy and people are healed, restored, cured of their infirmities, set free from their depressions, fears and burdens as they approach to receive prayer for healing. But the

Lord can and does heal sovereignly. He may do it at any point during the liturgy, before, during or after. Indeed, every Mass is healing because the Lord is always doing His works.

Personally, I have been involved in healing ministry since 1972 and I have witnessed countless miracles and healings through the ministry of Jesus. It is my great joy to be involved in this ministry of healing and I find that my particular ministry is to encourage expectant faith and to empower people to pray for healing. Often I minister through the Eucharist by preaching about Jesus who heals, giving some of my own life experiences and then dealing with some of the many blocks to receiving the Lord's healing action. These include unforgiveness, sense of unworthiness, fear, misunderstandings about redemptive suffering, offering it up, sense of rejection, focussing on the problem rather than on the Lord, control issues. People need to receive prayer when they are ready to receive, not when they are focussed on their needs. We encounter the healing Lord in the mystery of the Eucharist and then pray specifically for healing at the end of the celebration once we have turned from sin, focussed on Jesus and received Him in Communion. We allow Him to speak the word that heals us; we give Him permission to do so.

Frequently, in the ministry time I teach people to pray for healing. First, I have them get into groups of three and number off one-two-three. Then I tell number one that they will receive prayer for healing, number two leads the prayer, number three supports the prayer. Then I instruct each one. Number one tells Numbers two and three what the need for healing is. Numbers two and three lay a hand lightly on the shoulder of Number one. I instruct Number one to focus on the Lord, use their imagination to picture Jesus reaching out to heal them; give Jesus permission to do the healing; then receive – don't pray – just receive. Number three ministers the love of God and a healing touch, supporting the prayer of

Number two. Number two ministers the power of the Word of God with authority. Both Numbers two and three are to be open to vision or a word of encouragement, prophecy, word of wisdom/knowledge for the person for whom they just prayed. Then, after sharing the word or vision, they change places until each has a turn at receiving prayer, leading prayer and supporting prayer. The prayer led by Number two focusses that Jesus is the healer, a scripture on healing is brought to mind, then Jesus is asked to heal through the power of the Spirit. This is followed by the word of authority; in the name of Jesus Christ, be healed (set free, restored, made whole) for the Father's glory, the person's blessing, and the blessing of those they serve (the reasons for the healing).

There are many ways to lead healing ministry. But remember that Jesus is the healer. The more we are in intimate relationship, the more the power of the Spirit is evident in our lives. The more we approach Jesus with expectant faith, the more healing we receive through the Eucharist.

Chapter 6

PASTORAL APPLICATIONS

While the practice of medicine and science sees health as the absence of disease, faith in Jesus Christ sees health as a participation in the holiness or wholeness of the living God. Wholeness is holiness. In God there is no disease, illness or infirmity. The closer we come to the living God the more transformed we become. We are all born into the world with a weakened human nature because of the original sin of Adam and Eve and the constant build-up of the weight of sin growing in the world. Our personal sin adds to this weakened human condition.

Jesus Christ by his death and rising from the dead triumphed over sin and death, over the Evil One; and He established the Kingdom of God on earth. By baptism we enter into this kingdom of truth and justice, love and peace. We receive the grace-life of the Holy Spirit dwelling within us and as we learn to depend on the Holy Spirit we find ourselves growing in holiness and goodness. But we still live in the world in the midst of a culture of death that militates against our growth in holiness or wholeness.

Everywhere we see the need for healing to end the reign of disease and illness, infirmity and pain. So many people experience pain in their lives, from broken hearts, broken relationships, negative, destructive memories from childhood that are carried with them. I have never met a person who does not need some form of healing. Every parishioner, every person on the street, every generation: they all need healing, wholeness. The pain of sadness, loss, rejection, hatred, anger is everywhere. In the Lord there is found healing, the help needed to overcome, to have victory, to find peace and joy.

Jesus Christ said, "I have come so that they may have

life and have it to the full" (John 10:10). With abounding generosity He came to give us eternal life. The apostle Paul wrote: "The Spirit too comes to help us in our weakness" (Romans 8:26). He challenged the Corinthian Christian community and us:

> All the runners at the stadium are trying to win, but only one of them gets the prize. You must run in the same way, meaning to win. All the fighters at the games go into strict training; they do this just to win a wreath that will wither away, but we do it for a wreath that will never wither [eternal life]. That is how I run, intent on winning; that is how I fight, not beating the air. I treat my body hard and make it obey me, for, having been an announcer myself, I should not want to be disqualified (1 Corinthians 9:24-27).

"For anyone who is in Christ, there is a new creation" (2 Corinthians 5:17a). God who created all things through Christ has now restored His work, deformed by sin, by re-creating it in Christ. The central figure of this new creation is the "new man" created in Christ to lead a new life of virtue and holiness, of wholeness. The only Son of God, Jesus Christ, is both the source and the model of the way God has chosen for us to become holy.

> By his divine power, he has given us all the things that we need for life and for true devotion, bringing us to know God himself, who has called us by his own glory and goodness. In making these gifts, he has given us the guarantee of something very great and wonderful to come: through them you will be able to share the divine nature and to escape corruption in a world that is sunk in vice. But to attain this, you will have to do your utmost yourselves, adding goodness to the faith that you have, understanding to your goodness, self-control to your understanding, patience to your self-control, true devotion to your patience, kindness toward your fellow men to your devotion, and, to this kindness, love (2 Peter 1:3-6).

Living the Christian life in union with the Lord Jesus Christ brings life's greatest blessings: wholeness in the here and now and eternal life in the hereafter. Jesus did not know disease or illness in His life on earth but He did know persecution and suffering even though He was entirely whole. It can be the same for us as we live as God's children, breaking with sin, keeping the commandments, especially the law of love, and standing on guard against the enemies of Christ and against the world. "We belong to God but the whole world lies in the power of the Evil One" (1 John 5:19).

We need salvation, health, wholeness:

In *Community, Church and Healing*, physician R. A. Lambourne notes the frequency of healing works in the gospels. Five different Greek words express these healings. Two of them always describe medical healing, another means cleansing from leprosy, and another (rarely used) means "restore whole." The fifth Greek word for curing/healing is *sozein*. Its Latin version is *salus*, from which English derives both salvation and salve.

In scripture, while *sozein* refers to a medical situation, it is translated as healed or made whole. When used in a theological setting, it usually is translated as saved. Sozein is the word for curing/healing seen most often in the New Testament. If health means only physical wellness, why didn't the gospel writers use a word that means only medical healing? The writers deliberately chose an inclusive word because healing and salvation were so intertwined in Hebrew tradition and in the early church that they were nearly indistinguishable. "Salvation" meant health of body, mind and soul. We need to return to this truth and to remember that the church exists to bring us into health, into sozein in all its meanings.[16]

It was the Second Vatican Council (1962-1965) that restored the Sacrament of the Anointing of the Sick, giving it a new rite to reflect more closely the commission that Jesus gave to His disciples "to cure those who are sick" (Luke 10:9). Indeed, the Lord Himself showed His concern and care for the sick and directed His followers to do the same.

Even in our own day people do not understand healing ministry either through the sacrament or through the willing prayer of the disciples for healing. Many still fear the Anointing of the Sick, seeing in it the immediate end of life on earth since for so many centuries the sacrament was viewed as the last anointing, "Extreme Unction" as it was called.

Pastoral care of the sick is often limited in parishes, the Sacrament of Anointing only given when the nurse calls from the hospital that a person is close to death. The sacrament should be given in every serious illness when a person begins to be sick rather than waiting for the time when the illness is at the point of taking the person's life.

When I see the people in my parish I see that every single one of them has a need for healing, whether it is spiritual, medical, emotional, psychological or relational. How do we offer to people in the parish the experience of the healing ministry of Jesus Christ? It doesn't only occur in the Sacrament of the Anointing of the Sick but in a whole variety of ways as the Lord answers the prayer of those who turn to Him. The Lord may intervene directly or through any number of intermediate means to bring His loving, intimate care to a hurting person. Jesus directed all His disciples to bring God's healing touch to hurting people. In our parishes everyone needs to be formed or discipled in ministry to the sick.

While it is the priest who administers the sacrament of healing, the community of faith should participate so that they complement the priest's role and fulfill their own ministry of bringing healing to the sick by using their own gifts to support, bless and strengthen the sick by their loving attention, prayer and strength of faith that is expectant of the Lord's healing action. Whenever possible, the sacrament of anointing should be ministered in a community of faith context whether in an individual setting in hospital or home, or in a large gathering to minister to the many sick in the parish.

Healing services should occur in the parish at least once every three months. They may be held in a separate liturgy or in the context of the celebration of the Eucharist, either at a Mass set up for the particular purpose of ministering to the sick or at the regularly scheduled Masses on Sunday or weekday. But what about all the other people who are not suffering from life-threatening disease or illness? How do we minister to them? What about the personal suffering from deep sadness because of a broken heart, or the person with crippling arthritis, or the person who suffers from migraine headaches or the person with a skin disorder or the person with a broken ankle? The list can be endless. These people also need to receive and experience the healing love of Jesus Christ. How does the community of faith reach those who are in need?

Of course, faith for healing needs to be stirred up. People need to know that Jesus is the Healer. Expectant faith is absolutely necessary though the Lord does heal at times to give faith to the person who has no faith.

The *Catechism of the Catholic Church* tells us:

The Holy Spirit is "the principle of every vital and truly saving action in each part of the Body." He works in many ways to build up the whole Body in charity; by God's Word "which is able to build you up" (Acts 20:32); by Baptism, through which he forms Christ's Body; by the sacraments which give growth and healing to Christ's members; by the grace of the apostles, which holds first place among his gifts; by the virtues, which make us act according to what is good; finally, by the many specific graces (called "charisms") by which he makes the faithful "fit and ready to undertake various tasks and offices for the renewal and building up of the Church."[17]

Whether extraordinary or simple and humble, charisms are graces of the Holy Spirit which directly or indirectly benefit the Church, ordered as they are to her building up, to the good of men and to the needs of the world.[18]

Charisms are to be accepted with gratitude by the person who receives them, and by all members of the Church as well. They are a wonderfully rich grace for the apostolic vitality and for the holiness of the entire Body of Christ, provided they really are genuine gifts of the Holy Spirit and are used in full conformity with authentic promptings of this same Spirit, that is, in keeping with charity, the true measure of all charisms.[19]

The love of God is present in the world today and we witness it embodied in the brothers and sisters saved by Jesus Christ who are filled with the Spirit of Jesus. As people who are willing to serve, they use the charisms they have received. Through them Jesus continues to save and to heal humankind, renewing the whole world through the Spirit.

The pastoral care that every Christian Community must develop in its midst has this as its aim: to make people feel that they are no longer alone; that their past can not harm them with its memories and traumas. But first of all a Christian Community has to take care that men and women learn to make free and mature choices in the Holy Spirit.

This important learning can be obtained through physical and psychological healings experienced in answer to prayers, significantly in the Charismatic Community, as well as in others. It also comes from the fraternal love and care, especially that of spiritual directors, with whom we quietly "carry each other's burdens" (Galations 6:2).

These very important pastoral workers (many of them lay people) accompany their brothers and sisters on their spiritual journeys and teach them to look to Jesus: to receive direction from Him on how to deal with life's situations and choices, through prayer, prophecy and through seeking advice.... As they mature they rely on and trust God's will. This kind of experience, a new life in the Holy Spirit, is the strongest healing that anyone can have.[20]

Cardinal Joseph Bernardin wrote:

Our ministry will fall short of its desired effect unless we are faith-filled people; unless, in our own lives and ministry, we reflect the Lord and all his lovable qualities. People must see in us his love and mercy, his understanding and compassion.[21]

We need to know the Lord if we want to reflect or refract His presence in the world. A committed personal relationship with Jesus is absolutely essential if we are going to share the depth of our faith experience with others by ministering Jesus to them. It is Jesus who heals. It is by ministering Him that people experience and receive healing. Anyone who decides to minister healing to others will have to give of themselves, their time and energy, and the ministry can be very demanding, requiring lots of stamina and sacrifice. But deep, personal conversion is also necessary. To embrace holiness is to embrace Christ, dying to self and seeking intimacy with Jesus the Healer. None of us is holy enough or worthy enough to minister Jesus, but He chooses to use us as His vessels to bring love and healing to His wounded people. In spite of our unworthiness, in spite of our imperfection and sin, in spite of our mistakes, Jesus is revealed and people experience His healing action.

The Body of Christ is a community that has the power to heal but also the power to wound or cause pain. People are relational beings who require community to survive. From community, people develop moral values, religious ideas, attitudes toward health and sickness. In parishes and prayer communities where healing prayer teams are established, a powerful source of healing is available for the wounded members of the faith community.

A prayer team is set up with two or three, or even more,

people who believe that God has called them to minister, either as an individual or as a team, to bring the healing ministry of Jesus to those in need. They may pray for physical, spiritual, emotional, psychological or relational problems. The team is to make visible the healing presence of Jesus to the supplicants through the power of the love of Jesus who heals and sets free. The team ministers through the grace of hospitality, by exercising the blessing of pastoral listening, by stirring up expectant faith, modelling their own faith and giving witness to Jesus Christ. Led by or activated by the Holy Spirit, each time the team ministers they meet the supplicant where he or she is at, leading them to Jesus, making Jesus real to them so that He can meet the need expressed.

The place in which the members of the Body of Christ gather to focus on the need of the supplicant should be a sacred space in which they may experience an awareness of God's presence as they pray and worship God together. Key is to create the environment in which the supplicant can know God is really present to them in their need and that the illness can be healed, the disease cured and the need met. Team members need to be a team, having inner and outer peace, taking time for prayer, being willing to learn, seeking God's will and trusting in God. Of course, the supplicants must believe that the prayer team can and is willing to help them in their need as they cooperate with the grace of God in order to move towards wholeness and holiness.

Every parish should be a place of healing where people experience Jesus and are strengthened to continue on the journey of faith as they embrace the saving, healing love of the One who loves them. It is in and through the Church, the Body of Christ, that Jesus continues His healing ministry.

Chapter 7

FROM EXPERIENCE

I was ordained for the Hamilton diocese in Ontario in 1967. There had been nothing in my formation that prepared me to believe that Jesus heals today. In fact, even being asked in the hospital for my priestly blessing caused me some slight embarrassment. When different older people in the parish asked me on a Sunday morning to bless their eye or their knee, I was not aware of any particular change. It was simply something I did when the person asked.

Then, through a priest-friend, I was introduced to the Charismatic Renewal. I had seen the change in him; he had become a much more spiritual person. So I readily accepted prayer from a group of people at a prayer meeting. They laid hands on me and prayed for me to receive what is called the Baptism in the Holy Spirit. Some call it a release of the Spirit or an infilling of the Spirit's presence and power. But in reality it is the stirring up of the graces and gifts of the Spirit received in the sacraments of Baptism and Confirmation, and for me, in the sacrament of Holy Orders, since I was already an ordained priest. So many look at this Baptism in the Holy Spirit as something we need to receive, but the reality is that it occurs at the point in our lives when we give ourselves over to the Spirit. It is simply a turning away from sin towards the Lord, accepting Jesus as our personal Saviour and Lord and then asking Him to baptize us in the Spirit. The Spirit leads, guides, empowers and reveals Jesus to us. To be led by the Spirit is to walk in truth and goodness, depending on the Spirit, His presence and power active and visible in our lives.

My experience following being prayed with for this "Baptism" was one of great inner joy, incredible peace, a renewed prayer life and a tremendous enthusiasm for the

Spirit and the work of the Spirit. My experience at liturgy was that Jesus was visible and really present in the Eucharist and the other sacraments. Preaching became a joy. In short, it was as if I had become a new person. Expectant faith became a real part of my life and I began to experience the various charisms of the Spirit operative through others and through me (cf. 1 Corinthians 12:4-11).

It was another year before I became aware that the charism of healing was at work through me. While I had lots of expectant faith, it wasn't until I visited my priest-friend in Peru that I knew for certain that the Lord wanted to use me this way in ministry. Darryl, a young man from the parish where I was stationed at the time, accompanied me on this journey. The evening before we caught the plane for the journey he had injured his knee and the knee was heavily bandaged. After having walked a lot one afternoon in Lima, Darryl's knee began to cause him a great deal of pain. That night at dinner he asked me to pray with him for his knee. I said, "Sure. I'll get Jim and John" – the other two priests there. Darryl said, "No. Just you." After dinner we went into an adjoining room. Darryl sat down and I knelt. I placed my hands on his knee and began to pray. It seemed that Darryl's knee began to move inside, under my hands, and a line from scripture went through my head: "Walking and leaping and praising God" (Acts 3:8), taken from the cure of a lame man at the Beautiful Gate in Jerusalem.

I thought, "Peter, you have to step out in faith." I said, "Darryl, take off the bandage and walk; your knee is fine" and I was hoping all the time that is was. Darryl took off the bandage and literally danced the rest of the night. The rest, as they say, is history. I talked to my friend Jim and he confirmed that he believed God was giving me a healing ministry. I spent the next three weeks in Peru praying for healing ... a dying baby was immediately well and began to take nourishment, a blind lady received her sight, a woman who had had miscarriage after miscarriage and had never brought a child to term was instantly visibly changed before our eyes, and in due course delivered a healthy baby. It seems that in the climate of simple and expectant faith, everything we asked in prayer was received.

Then, returning home to Canada, I found that expectant faith was not a popular commodity. Most of our Catholic people did not expect God to intervene in a concrete way to bring healing and relief from pain: They prayed but not with expectant faith for the moment. Rather, belief was that they would eventually get better or that they had to rely on drugs or medical treatment, surgery or long-term physiotherapy. They just had to "offer it up," bear with it, since that was their lot in life. Prayer was not considered to be effective, but we had to pray anyway because that was how we kept on the "right side of God." However, there were always exceptions – people who had some experience of God's healing intervention.

Having returned to parish ministry in Canada, I first experienced divine healing when I dropped by to bless a parishioner's home. The lady who met me at the door had broken a finger while moving furniture and she was just going to the doctor. However, she invited me in for a few minutes. We talked and prayed together as I lightly held the broken finger in my hand. We watched the swelling go down, the discolouration leave, flexibility return to the finger as all the pain disappeared. She had faith because she had seen her mother-in-law restored to health when she had received the Sacrament of the Anointing of the Sick while in intensive care. Her mother-in-law was well enough to go home the next day. The lady with the broken finger, at my direction, went to see her doctor anyway and was told there was nothing wrong with her finger.

Thus began my healing ministry in Canada – through the celebration of what are called "Healing Masses" and through individual ministry. Of course, healing can take place in any Mass. After all, in every Mass before we receive Communion we pray, "Only say the word and I shall be healed." In Healing Masses prayer is specifically offered for healing of all kinds of sickness and infirmity. Over the last thirty years I have had the opportunity to teach and preach and minister healing in a wide variety of situations in different countries. God is so good and so faithful. Jesus is the healer and He continues to minister healing to His people today.

Prayer for healing may be offered for many different needs, whether physical, emotional, spiritual, psychological or relational. There are many different forms of ministry that have been developed to meet particular needs in the Church. Whether prayer is offered by a small child, by a team of two or three people who pray together for the supplicant, or by someone leading the ministry in a large group gathering – Jesus is present and active through the power of the Holy Spirit.

I remember one man who told me how he had badly stubbed his toe and was in excruciating pain. His young son ran and got the bottle of blessed oil, put some on his dad's big toe and said, "Jesus, heal daddy's toe." Instantly, the pain disappeared and the toe was healed. Such is the expectant faith of a small child. Another time, I remember two men with elbow problems who were part of a larger group of people who were experiencing pain at the moment. As I led prayer the people, one after another, experienced the pain disappear. One of the men with the elbow problem was pain-free instantly – in fact, three times during the course of the week he told me that he loved me because of what I had done for his elbows. The other man with the elbow problem experienced no change in his condition. We prayed with him three times. Finally, I asked him what the block was that was stopping the healing from taking place. He responded, "I don't know. Everyone here was in such pain; I was just offering it up for them." That was the block to healing. He had chosen to suffer the pain and let it be beneficial for the others who were suffering. He was disappointed that the healing didn't occur for himself, but he had chosen to bear the pain. We don't always understand the Lord's ways.

Sometimes healings are very simple responses to prayer; at other times they seem to be very dramatic. The Lord can equally and easily take away a headache or raise someone from the dead. Once, having just sustained a concussion in a fall, I went to Edmonton, Alberta, to speak on a Friday evening to a gathering of five hundred people. In spite of my condition, I knew the Lord wanted me to speak on healing that evening. During my talk I had a strong sense that the Lord was healing people spontaneously as I spoke. In response to my request for a show of hands as to how many had received healing that night since they had gathered, about two hundred and fifty hands went up. To conclude the evening, I offered prayer for healing with the anointing of blessed oil. Through the crowd I saw a man being held up by three people. Immediately I thought of the paralytic being lowered to the feet of Jesus (cf. Mark 2:1-12). I moved through the crowd and anointed the man on the forehead with the blessed oil as I prayed in Tongues. I sensed Jesus say to me, "He has the faith to be healed." I opened my eyes and looked at him. All I saw was a dead, limp body being supported by his three friends. I closed my eyes as I continued to pray in Tongues. Immediately, Jesus said, "He will be healed as they move away." I simply turned and walked back to the people lined up for prayer and anointing. But I kept watching for what would happen. After a few minutes, they began to move away and I lost sight of them in the crowd. Then the hall was suddenly filled with cries of "Alleluia!" and "Praise God!" as the crowd parted to reveal the man leaping, jumping, dancing, talking a blue streak, as his cane went flying and joy burst from him. Going back to him, I learned that he had been the victim of massive head injuries in a car accident six years earlier. The Lord had miraculously restored him, completely healing him. I continue to be filled with delight as I experience the wonders our God can do with even a tiny bit of faith.

To pray for physical healing we simply ask and receive. It is sometimes difficult to encourage the expectant faith needed for the Lord to act. In my experience, I have found more faith for healing when someone comes asking "in faith" for the healing to take place. It is a different story altogether when one goes to offer prayer for healing. For example, to visit shut-ins in seniors' homes or nursing homes, or in private homes, prayer can be offered for healing and the person then responds, "That was very nice, Father. Would you like a cup of tea?"

The expectation of healing is not always easy to stir into existence; in fact, many believe the Lord can heal but won't heal them or that it will happen eventually. But I have ministered healing in a large gathered group in a seniors' home where many expressed that healing had taken place. I remember one lady whose whole personality seemed to change instantly for the better, another who walked off without her walker, a man in a wheelchair whose pain in the leg instantly disappeared. Healing happens in so many ways.

Tremendous spiritual healing takes place through the Sacrament of Reconciliation wherein a person experiences the release of their burden, a freeing of their own spirit, peace of heart and mind, soul and spirit, as they have turned to the Lord, allowing themselves to become a new creation, a new person. Sometimes, physical healing also occurs. Often, doubt, anxiety, fear, worry disappear as hope and trust fill the person's heart. Spiritual healing takes place every time we move closer to the Lord, turning from sin, letting go of the sadness that burdens our spirits. Spiritual healing so often follows an experience of the presence and action of the Lord God because faith and confidence in God develop.

Emotional or psychological healing have as their root a deep wound from rejection or pain that has been inflicted on a person's soul or spirit. It is one thing to be burdened with one's own sin and negative behaviour, and another to be the victim of the sin or destructive behaviour of another. Those who have soul/spirit hurts often need to receive a ministry of healing called "inner healing," "healing of memories" or "healing of soul/spirit hurts."

A person may experience guilt or shame. Guilt says, "I have done something wrong." Shame says, "I am wrong." Guilt and shame may be self-inflicted or be inflicted by others. A common way to come to healing is by allowing a team of two or three trained and prepared people to pray with you over a period of two or three appointments. During this period the team who fasts and prays, listens and discerns, leads the individual into freedom and healing. The process is usually by praying chronologically through the person's life from the moment of conception through to the present moment, as the team seeks to discern the root and cause of the pain the person is experiencing. Involved may be a sense of inadequacy, of inferiority, of fear, anger, hatred, of rebellion, of abandonment, loss or betrayal, of rejection or a host of other negative experiences that have marked the person for a life of pain or bondage. It is Jesus, invited by prayer and the faculty of the imagination, who heals as the wounded person forgives whomever has caused the pain or the wound in their past. As the root is discovered and healed, the person is freed to take up their life in joy and peace, in wholeness.

A common experience when an inner healing ministry begins is that the person receiving ministry has flashbacks of incidents in their life that need forgiveness and healing. When forgiveness is given sincerely from the heart, Jesus can heal the wound that is there.

Of course, whatever is mentioned or prayed for in this ministry is to be kept strictly confidential. Other charisms of the Spirit in addition to various gifts of healing may be operative. The Word of Knowledge will often diagnose or reveal the root of the problem; the Word of Wisdom will give direction as to what to do with what is diagnosed; the charism of Prophecy will speak the Lord's mind and heart into the situation; the use of the charism of Tongues will either speak directly to the spirit of the person being prayed with or will address hidden issues not dealt with in the vernacular prayer.

Sometimes, intergenerational prayer for healing is required as the prayer team discovers similar patterns in previous generations of the particular family tree. Just as a person can inherit a particular physical trait or weakness, they can inherit or receive a negative characteristic or a particular openness to evil influence. For example, a tendency to alcoholism can be passed down from one generation to the next; in every generation there can be individuals who make the same wrong decisions as their forebears; there can be the same negative conditioning passed from one generation to the next. In one family tree there may be only people who are good and righteous, successful in career and quality of life, whereas in another there may be constant struggle, limited educational achievement, poverty, poor quality of life, moral weakness and frequent difficulties with law and order. It may well be that healing, involving forgiveness and the decision to live free in the Lord, is the route to change the negative cycle for this generation and the ones to follow.

The more time we give to the enemy the less we give to the Lord. But it is true that we live in the midst of spiritual warfare, that the enemy is always actively seeking to destroy us, incapacitate us, weaken the grace-life within us. It is necessary to know our enemy, the devil and his demons, their tricks and ways of operating, their tactics and ways of thinking and attacking. We need to wear the full armour of God, be watchful and ready, live a life of grace and goodness, of obedience to the will of God. However, the reality is that often people simply open their lives to the evil one so that he can enter, or people drop their defenses and the enemy begins to take control. The enemy can harass his victim externally or may gain entrance to a person's life through sin or foolish curiosity. Deliverance ministry, which is actually part of the inner-healing ministry, refers specifically to setting people free who are bound by the power of evil, either through obsession, bondage or partial possession. Exorcism is reserved to the power of the Church with the authority of the bishop invested in a particular priest for the freeing of a trapped soul from full possession. It is only after every other possibility is considered that the Church may allow an exorcism to take place.

In these days, the presence and power of God is being manifested more and more. Yet at the same time we witness a concurrent rise of evil as the reign of God is being established on earth. But many countless numbers of people have fallen victim to the evil one. There is a major challenge to heal and restore people to wholeness and goodness. That is one of the reasons the healing ministry of Jesus Christ is so necessary in the Church and world today. The Lord does care, and through His healing ministry He offers a way to wholeness and transformation of life. The Lord wants the whole person to be healed; He wants to overcome the effects of past hurts; He wants to meet His people in their needs because He is full of love and compassion for His people.

The Charismatic Renewal is the spirituality of the Church. It is not just a movement like other movements. It is a singular grace of Almighty God following the Second Vatican Council to give faith to those searching for the truth in all the wrong places. This renewal has brought healing to the fore once again as it was in the Early Church and at various times down through history.

From my own experience, I can testify to the wondrous blessings of the Lord given in response to prayer. Whether by anointing with oil, the laying on of hands, a direct word of command, the use of a relic from a saint, whether as part of a prayer team or acting alone in the power of the Spirit, the Lord ministers healing leading to wholeness of body, mind and spirit. He reveals His loving presence and care for His people.

But good people can still be fearful of the Lord's action. Just yesterday I preached about my own experiences of how the Lord multiplied food in response to prayer to meet the need. Afterwards a woman spoke to me, telling me her own experience of how the Lord answered her prayer to multiply the food. The Lord did. Amazed at the Lord's response to "her miracle," she still found the whole thing "creepy." It is difficult for many people to realize that the Lord is really that close, hearing and answering the prayer we bring to Him. To trust the Lord is the single biggest challenge people have in life. To invite Jesus to be the Lord and centre of one's life is a simple but major step in faith and trust. When we do so and then begin to ask the Lord to provide for our needs as we place our trust in Him, amazing answers to prayer fill our lives. The same Jesus who walked through Galilee and saw and met the needs of the people who came to Him is still doing the same today.

Chapter 8

PRACTICAL PROCEDURES
IN DIFFERENT MINISTRY FORMS

The imposition of hands, known as the laying on of hands, is present in all of the sacraments. In Baptism, after the anointing with the Oil of the Saints, hands are laid on the head of the one being baptized. In Confirmation, the laying on of hands is done by the one doing the confirming, although in large groups the extending of the hands is done over all those to be confirmed at the same time. In the sacrament of Reconciliation the celebrant is to impose hands over the penitent as the penitent receives absolution. In Eucharist the priest imposes hands over the bread and wine that is to be changed into the Body and Blood of Jesus Christ, and the minister of communion is to lightly touch the hand of the person receiving as Communion is placed on the palm of the hand. In Holy Orders, the bishop and all priests present lay hands on the head of the one being ordained. In Marriage in which the couple give the sacrament to each other, they join their right hands and declare their consent; the celebrant then places his hand over theirs to conclude the rite of exchanging consent. In the sacrament of Anointing of the Sick, the priest lays hands on the sick person while silently inviting the healing action of the Spirit.

The laying on of hands is the traditional way of passing on the Spirit. It is a sacrament of touch. In pastoral care, touch is essential. In fact, we are called and created to touch. A newborn baby would not survive without the touch of love. The body was made to give and receive touch and touch is necessary to sustain life, wholeness, balance and peace. The sense of self or wholeness requires touch and it is necessary to build relationships and community. We need only watch a parent with their newborn child to see how important touch is. We observe the touch of companionship when people walk together holding hands, when people get excited at a sports event or when the team wins. People shake hands or give a hug on meeting or leaving. When someone is frightened or sick or upset, how important touch is to bring calm, healing, peace. Touch is really part of heart/hand coordination. The touch expresses what is in the heart. The touch of love or support brings joy and strength.

In the Old Testament the Jewish people were given strict laws about touch. They could not touch or be touched by a leper or they would become ritually unclean. Yet Jesus touched the lepers and made them whole. About one-fifth of the Gospel accounts detail the healing ministry of Jesus. In Acts 3:7 we are told that Peter "took him by the hand and helped him to stand up" and the lame man was healed. Jesus by His own example showed the value of the healing touch, the laying on of hands and the word of command for healing to take place.

There are, though, still many people who do not like to be touched; sometimes that is cultural conditioning or it may be fear of being contaminated or misunderstood. It could also be a hesitancy to trust the other. Whatever it is, the minister of healing should be sensitive to the supplicant, not forcing unwelcome touch. It is best to ask permission to lay hands for healing so that the recipient is relaxed and receptive. Healing is always a process. A reserve or lack of trust in one area can affect healing in another.

Healing touch is an integral part of healing ministry. It is the touch of Jesus who is truly loving and compassionate; it is Jesus reaching out to bring wholeness to His beloved. For a person to know that they have been touched by Jesus is to produce joy and increased faith in their life, even changed behaviour and growth in holiness.

Many of our congregations experience limited touch

except at the exchange of peace during the celebration of the Eucharist. Without touch, worship tends to remain a very individual experience even in the midst of a crowd. Our congregations need more by way of experience of the presence of the living God. It would be wonderful to reshape our liturgy to include healing touch. Every baptized person has a role to play in the life and outreach of the People of God bringing healing, compassion, forgiveness and peace to others.

The Early Church was built not just by teaching and preaching but also by signs and wonders as people experienced the healing, freeing ministry of Jesus Christ. Jesus is alive, raised from the dead, and is working in the present and is changing, transforming lives.

Luke Timothy Johnson in his book entitled *Religious Experience in Earliest Christianity* states:

> As I have suggested, the historical critical paragon – in its older and newer forms – is not only impatient with the category of experience, it does not know what to do with it, almost inevitably shifting away from attention to the particular toward some sort of developmental scheme. The same is true of the so-called New Testament theology, which maintains its precarious existence precisely by suppressing the specificity of the text and their capacity to surprise. Both the historical and theological paragons – at least as usually practised – tend toward the general and abstract, whereas this religious language remains specific and concrete.... I argue that serious engagement with earliest Christianity demands recognition that its adherents had quite another view; they consider themselves caught up by, defined by a power not in their control but rather controlling them, a power that derived from the crucified and risen Messiah, Jesus. Indeed, I am convinced that any effort to interpret the writings of early Christianity (I am thinking of non-canonical as well as canonical literature) that does not proceed on

this assumption is fated to fall short of a satisfying interpretation.[22]

In a summary entitled "A Working Definition of Religious Experience," Luke Timothy Johnson lists:

1. Religious experience is a response to what is perceived as ultimate.
2. Religious experience involves the whole person.
3. Religious experience is characterized by peculiar intensity.
4. Religious experience issues in action.[23]

Johnson gives the example of Saul's conversion to become Paul the Apostle as a classic example of religious experience in the full sense of the definition. He writes:

> It is well known that the accounts in the Acts of the Apostles and Paul's letters do not entirely overlap and it is impossible to trace out completely the specific, somatic, psychic, or symbolic dimensions of what seeing the Lord Jesus months or years after Jesus' execution might have been. But what the accounts in all of Paul's activities do make clear is that whether sudden or slow, whether spectacular or subtle, this encounter completely restructured his life, and for that matter, the life of much of the world.[24]

He concludes the chapter by writing:

> If scholarship cannot speak in an accurate and disciplined fashion about the experiential aspects of earliest Christianity, then it misses what is most interesting, and quite likely what is most distinctive about this puzzling and paradoxical religious movement.[25]

Current Christianity is still a practical, concrete experiencing of the risen Lord who encounters, heals and transforms His people. It is the experience that changes lives and changes hearts, not abstract statements of theology. The challenge to us today is how to lead people into the experience of Jesus who saves and heals. It is time to be creative in Church liturgy and worship, in service and outreach, providing opportunities for people to encounter Jesus in His loving, healing touch.

Many who offer prayer ministry for healing do so following the celebration of a Healing Mass or a prayer meeting. The word of God is proclaimed in the preaching, expectant faith stirred up. Communion for oneness with Jesus and His Body is received and the supplicant readies their heart to receive the Lord's ministry. Usually people tell the prayer team what they are asking to receive. One of the team anoints the supplicant with blessed oil as a sign of strength and healing through the Spirit of Jesus. (Sometimes this oil which is a sacramental is referred to as the "oil of gladness.") Then the team members lay hands on the head, shoulder or hands of the recipient as the team leader leads the prayer. The other team members will pray in their prayer language of Tongues and may give a prophecy or a word of encouragement, a word of knowledge or wisdom, or simply share a vision that they receive during the prayer. The prayer time need not be long; short and simple is best, although at times an extended period of prayer, called "soaking prayer," is applicable. Jesus is the Healer and so the healing does not depend on the length of the prayer or the team members "getting it right." Keep it simple, focussed on Jesus. Ask and receive.

In ministry I have tried to be creative, ministering or leading ministry in different ways. Key to all healing ministry is to get the person to take their eyes off the problem and to look at the Lord. Often I minister in larger groups with a simple laying on of hands while I pray quietly in Tongues. I encourage the people to speak to the Lord and tell Him what they need before they leave their pews. I can't do anything about their particular need or list of needs – only Jesus can; so tell Him! I encourage the people to stand at the foot of the sanctuary in a single line across the front, facing the altar. Then I ask them to close their eyes, focus their attention on Jesus, open their hearts to Him, give Him permission to do the healing, open their hands to receive, don't pray, just receive. Then I simply move from one to the other, lightly touching finger tips as I pray in the Spirit. The prayer is very brief for each one, but the presence and power of the Lord is very evident. Some are jolted as if shocked by electricity; others fall to the ground completely relaxed and at peace until the overwhelming sense of the Lord's love passes; others experience love, refreshment, pain disappearing, inner peace or joy. Not everyone experiences a physical or emotional sensation, but many do, knowing they have been touched by the Lord Jesus. Some just simply know their need has been met.

But there are always some who are more interested in what is happening around them, or wondering when their turn for prayer is, or are simply curious. When a person is not focussed, receptive to meeting and receiving from the Lord, they miss their opportunity. However, the Lord can still heal such a one in order to give faith.

I have also arranged other kinds of healing services that have been tremendously effective. It is important, I believe, to take advantage of the local church structure and its furnishings. For example, at Holy Cross Church in Regina, Saskatchewan, there was a large sanctuary with stairs in the centre leading to the sanctuary platform and other stairs leading up to the large stone altar which was situated in front of a large stone crucifix that extended from floor to ceiling. In prayer, I sensed a "prayer ladder" and so I asked the ten members of the national Charismatic committee to minister in pairs forming a ladder up to the altar. The people came forward for ministry, individually passing through the five teams who spoke prophecy, vision, words of knowledge and wisdom, or prayed specifically for healing. The effect was so powerful that people had to be helped up the stairs. When the people arrived at the altar, they were to lay their hands on the altar and offer their lives to Jesus, then turn and embrace the stone crucifix to crucify all their sinful passions and desires. When they came down the steps on the other side of the altar, it was with joy, freedom and tremendous healing – even those who had walked with canes didn't need them. I stood at the end of the journey to embrace or touch and greet them, as appropriate, with the Father's love. Another variation is to have people go to the baptismal font and touch or place their hands in the water for cleansing and renewal.

Another kind of healing service is to provide a variety of options at the same time, allowing people the opportunity to take advantage of each ministry offered. With the Blessed Sacrament exposed in the monstrance, people are encouraged to go the Lord directly and, while touching the base of the monstrance, ask the Lord for whatever miracle they need. At the same time, the opportunity is available for private confession. In the same service, another ministry of healing is offered: a team of people representing God, self and others stands and welcomes people who choose to forgive. In the sacrament of Reconciliation we are forgiven, but we need opportunities so that we can forgive those who have hurt us. The team members represent or stand in the place of God the Father, clergy, religious, parents (both mother and father), the elderly, youth, self (both male and female) and others (again, both male and female representatives). That gives people a wonderful opportunity to express forgiveness when they are not normally able to do so, perhaps because someone has died or they don't have the courage to directly confront the one who has hurt them. They may go to any or all of the team members as they have need. The team member stands with open hands to welcome the one coming to forgive. The team member, making the sign of the cross on the person's forehead, says, "I love you; I forgive you. Please forgive me." The person responds, "I forgive you." Then the team member enfolds the person in a loving embrace and holds it until the one asking forgiveness breaks it. There is to be no backpatting. That is done to burp babies or it is very common in sports' celebrations of victory to back slap. But I understand it to mean "I don't trust you" when it is given as a loving embrace. The ministry here is to offer unconditional love which produces wonderful healing of wounds. Of course, tears flow freely. Tears are the cleansing of the soul, a releasing of the burden, a freeing of the spirit, joy and happiness. It has been my experience that the ones offering this ministry are greatly blessed as they experience God's merciful love pass through them. It is wise to choose people who are good huggers to do this ministry so that the recipient experiences unconditional love.

It is a wonderful thing to be able to empower people so that they recognize and know that the power of God's love to heal and to set free flows through them. In parish healing Masses in my own parish, I would regularly ask people to assist with the ministry of the laying of hands when they themselves had not done so before. Always, they were somewhat overwhelmed to experience God working through them. I know that at times people are very cautious about who leads the prayer ministry for healing or who participates as a team member in the ministry. When the pastoral authority is present there is not a need to fear the ministry being given under that authority. For people to be trained in healing ministry is excellent, but prayer for healing should not be limited to those who are trained. All can pray for healing and should be taught how to do so, but the parish or prayer group may limit who officially represents them in ministry outreach.

One of the best ways to offer healing ministry is to involve everyone in giving and receiving prayer for healing. This can work effectively in a very large or a small group of people. Divide people into groups of three and, in turn, let them each receive prayer, lead the prayer or support the prayer. The one receiving the prayer is encouraged to tell the other two in their group what their healing need is, then to close their eyes (so that they are not distracted), open their heart to Jesus, focus their attention on Him, give Him permission to do the healing, picture Him reaching out to touch and to heal, be aware of His presence, then not to pray but to simply receive. They may experience something like electricity flowing through them, a deep peace, pain disappearing, full movement being restored, tremendous heat from those laying hands on them, a warmth passing through their body, a vision, a prophetic word, a clear direction from the Lord or they may simply and clearly just know that the Lord is with them. The one leading the prayer should just be aware of the Lord's presence and picture Jesus reaching out to heal as they speak the word of authority or command. The one who supports the ministry, also with the laying on of hands, ministers the Lord's love with a healing touch. As an open vessel of the Lord's love and healing, they let the Lord's love flow through their hands and heart to the person receiving prayer, as they desire with everything in their being as the most important thing in the world at this moment the healing of the brother or sister for whom they pray. Aware of the Lord's presence with them, they picture Jesus reaching out to heal and may picture the healing actually taking place.

As the one leading this ministry – three times so each gets a turn – I lead the prayer in which I have the leader of each group repeat after me. In the prayer I focus on Jesus as the Healer, use a scripture to support the healing and then give the word of authority or command speaking to the people's needs. I try to vary the prayer so that we don't get caught in a particular formula for prayer. A typical prayer could be:

Lord Jesus Christ, You are the Healer. All things are possible with You. Stretch out Your hand and heal. Work your Signs and wonders to bring healing to my brother (sister). Minister in the power of Your Holy Spirit to bring the fullness of healing, to meet the needs expressed as I speak Your word of authority, Your word of command. In the name of the Lord Jesus Christ, be healed. In the name of the Lord Jesus Christ, be set free. In the name of the Lord Jesus Christ, come into the fullness of health and restoration, for the Father's glory, for your blessing, and for the blessing of all those you serve. In the name of Jesus Christ be it done. Thank you, Jesus. Praise you, Jesus. How holy is Your name. Alleluia!

There can be many other variations of liturgy or healing service set up to meet the needs of people. My whole focus in ministry is to raise expectant faith and to empower people for ministry. The more that are involved in healing ministry, the more the work of the Lord can take place, leading people to deep, abiding faith and trust in the Lord Jesus Christ who is the Healer. I do try to keep the focus on Jesus, not on myself, since He is the Healer, not I. It is the healing ministry of Jesus Christ that is continuing in the Church today through faith-filled disciples who reveal Jesus to the nations by focussing His loving, compassionate touch on those who are in need.

Chapter 9

POSSIBLE DANGERS, ABUSES, ABERRATIONS IN HEALING MINISTRY

The greatest single danger for the minister of healing is to neglect one's personal prayer life. A lack of prayer indicates a diminished relationship with the Lord. Since all ministry of the Spirit flows from a dynamic relationship of commitment to the Lord and His service, there must be time spent in private prayer. This way was certainly the way for Jesus, our model in ministry, who took time to withdraw by Himself to spend time with His heavenly Father. It was in this way that He kept on track with His Father's will and blessing, that He knew the Spirit's leading and empowerment.

Sometimes a healing minister allows his prayer to be only that of praying for others or praying with others in a group, for example, at the prayer meeting. This is not sufficient to keep him fresh and alive in ministry. It is in the quiet place of one's heart that one experiences the Lord's revelation and clarity for ministry. To learn to listen reaps the greatest blessings. Presumption of the Lord's empowerment can lead to disaster, though the Lord can and does minister through the circumstances to the faithful who trust in Him. Often I am amazed at those who consider themselves to be healers when there is only one healer – Jesus Christ, the Son of the living God. When a person operates in their own power they set themselves up for a fall that can destroy their ministry.

Sometimes a healing minister concentrates so much on self that they lose the whole sense of the ministry of Jesus through the Church, and that is the ministry of the Body of Christ, people ministering to each other as part of their baptismal walk in faith. It is readily apparent when there is too much "I" and not enough "we" in the minister's presentation of healing. That can lead to too much individualism wherein the healing minister is the only one able to minister because he/she has all the power. This attitude contradicts First Corinthians, Chapter 12, where Paul speaks using the analogy of the body with all its parts working together in proper order to explain how the variety of gifts operate in unity.

At times, people seek to escape the ministry of healing entrusted to them because they don't want the responsibility or the attention. This person may be lacking in boldness or courage, being fearful, doubtful, uncertain or underestimating God's desire to use them in ministry. In the Church, ministry is an obligation, not an option. There can be a residual doubt in the person about the authority, ability or willingness of the Lord to minister into the situation or to minister through this "unworthy" minister. But none of us are worthy, and God chooses to use us anyway.

The healing minister should have a passionate desire to do God's will and a passionate desire to learn. Some people are simply unteachable: they know everything already; it's either their way or the highway. Oh, how blessed it is to have people eager to learn the Lord's ways, willing to take instruction and being open to constructive criticism so that they can learn from their mistakes to minister more effectively and with the Lord's compassion.

A healing minister can get caught up in pursuing their own agenda rather than the Lord's. To be part of a healing ministry requires obedience to the leadership and the willingness to minister as directed by the one in charge of the overall ministry for the common good. It can be easy for a prayer minister to get caught into moralizing or giving advice when part of their role is to focus the supplicants to trust the Lord and look to Him for the revelation of His answer to prayer. Sometimes the one leading the prayer can over-identify with the one to whom they are ministering and this is because the one ministering is not emotionally whole – they need to withdraw from the ministry and seek healing for themselves before they return to ministry.

Discernment is critical. Sometimes the minister may simply be lacking in this charism of the Spirit or may uncritically use this gift of discernment. This can happen, for example, when a person ministering receives what is known as a word of knowledge or a revelation. To simply state as a fact what they received, for example: "You were raped at the age of twelve" can be very destructive, causing all kinds of barriers to go up in defense. It is much better to use the word of knowledge in a non-aggressive way, asking: "Did you have a traumatic experience when you were about twelve years old?" This allows freedom to the individual receiving ministry to open the wound for healing.

A lack of discernment concerning those who claim to have the gift of healing can also open the door to destruction. Anyone can pray for healing but unknown people who visit and want to minister in a particular prayer group should be discerned by the appointed or elected leadership as to the validity of the ministry and its appropriateness at the time. There have been many who have suffered because an itinerant ministry has shown up unannounced and been allowed to minister. This can be particularly destructive with itinerant deliverance ministries who can cause great upset, misunderstanding and leave a trail of broken, messed-up people behind. Discernment is a valuable charism of the Spirit given to protect and serve right order so that those discerning know what spirit is operative: the Holy Spirit, the evil spirit or the human spirit or which combination of spirits. Believe me, the human spirit is far more operative than we could imagine.

It is truly unfortunate that there is not more training available for people to learn how to minister divine healing. People generally tend to gather with certain personalities who corner the "healing market." This amounts to personality cults and people seek out the "known healers" to receive healing when the healing power of Jesus is available right where they are at the moment if they would just turn to Him.

It is good to have people work together in pairs, changing partners when appropriate. Remember that there is no one set format or way that ministry is to be done or one particular way that works. It is the ministry of Jesus to His people and we share the ministry with Him. Even as we offer prayer with others for healing we experience healing ourselves.

Those who are chosen or asked to minister healing in a particular group should have a solid, emotionally well-balanced spiritual life, a love of people and an ability to take direction, be teachable and have a desire to grow in the ministry of healing. The members of the team will need to study healing and the scriptures, be under spiritual direction and agree to being under supervision.

QUESTIONS THAT ARISE IN HEALING MINISTRY

1. Does everyone get healed?

While our desire is that all get healed at the time of prayer, this is not always the case. Sometimes the healing happens gradually, a steady improvement taking place. A person may not realize the healing has taken place until days, weeks or months later. While scripture tells us that Jesus healed all who came to Him (Matthew 4:24, 8:16; Mark 1:32; Luke 6:18-19), there were also special times when Jesus experienced that "the power of the Lord was behind his works of healing (Luke 5:17). At the pool of Bethzatha, Jesus healed only one man yet there were many present in need of healing (John 5:1-20). When Jesus had crowds come to Him to be healed, He would withdraw privately "where he could be alone and pray" (Luke 5:15,16). When we pray, some form of healing always happens for those who ask with faith. It may not be what was specifically requested, but the Lord does answer the prayer in some way.

2. Does healing happen instantly?

While most of the healings recorded in the New Testament happened instantly at the word or touch of Jesus (Mark 1:31,42), He at times prayed twice as, for example, the blind man at Bethsaida (Mark 8:22-26) who gradually came to have clear sight. Healing is a process whereas a miracle is an instant transformation. Some healings are miracles, others take place in a speeded-up process. For example, a lady I know had badly broken her ankle in a fall over a skateboard. Her doctor told her it was going to take six months before she could walk again. After prayer she was walking with a completely restored ankle in six weeks' time.

3. After a person receives prayer, should the use of medicine be discontinued?

The use of medicine should be continued until the doctor discontinues it. God who is the source of all healing uses various means to bring it about. Chapter 38 of Ecclesiasticus (Sirach) has a beautiful section on the role of prayer and the role of the physician and the pharmacist.

4. Is having faith necessary to receive healing?

While not necessary, it certainly helps. Expectant faith can receive much. The person requesting prayer for healing may have expectant faith to be healed. It may be that the person who offers the prayer may be the one who has the expectant faith necessary for the healing action of the Lord to be present. It may be the faith of another who intercedes for the sick person. Or, it may be that the Lord simply heals without any real expectation on the part of the one praying or the one being prayed with. It may simply be that they are in a climate of faith wherein the Lord works sovereignly to give faith to the one who is healed. Remember, too, that expectant faith is not the same as the virtue of faith. Expectant faith is the kind of faith that can move mountains and is actually the charism of faith at work.

5.   Is there a particular way to pray for healing?

No. The way to pray for healing is as varied as the individual who prays. The prayer should be simple and clear, giving the Lord Jesus permission to do the healing necessary for the blessing of the person in need so that God is glorified and the person healed is blessed as well as those whom they serve or to whom they witness God's love and mercy. There is no method that works all the time. Whatever the prayer, it should flow from the heart and be sincere, placing trust and confidence in Jesus to answer the need for the greatest good of the person receiving prayer.

6.   Does someone become a "healer" when a person prayed for is healed?

No. Jesus is the only healer. Healing is the power, love and compassion of the Lord at work in people's lives. The person who prays and sees good results from their prayer is God's instrument and may have a ministry of healing led by the Spirit of God. Key to the ministry is to bring the recipients of prayer face to face, as it were, with Jesus who reaches out to heal and set free, make new and transform the recipients, bringing wholeness into their lives. While anyone can pray for healing either for themselves or for others and experience healing, some are given the ministry of healing to extraordinary degree. While people may refer to them as healers, it still remains that Jesus is the healer and they are the instruments or vessels of love and power that the Lord uses to minister to His people.

7.   Is sin always the cause of sickness?

Sickness may be the result of the person's own sinfulness, unforgiveness, improper diet, lack of exercise, etc., so not all sickness is directly caused by sin. The Old Testament has much to say about blessing and curse. To keep covenant with God was to live in the blessing, to break covenant was to be cursed (cf. Deuteronomy 28:1-68). The New Testament speaks of the connection between sin and sickness, for example, in the letter of James 5:15-16: "The prayer of faith will save the sick man and the Lord will raise him up again; and if he has committed any sins, he will be forgiven. So confess your sins to one another, and pray for one another, and this will cure you."

8. Are suffering and sickness given to us by God?

In the Scriptures there is no indication that Jesus was ever sick. He was tired, hungry and thirsty, and He was persecuted. Suffering and sickness are not synonymous terms. The Christian may suffer persecution but sickness is not God's will. Jesus is the healer and God's will is to make whole, to heal, to have perfect harmony and goodness in the life of every Christian.

In Peter's address in the house of Cornelius, he says of Jesus, "God had anointed him with the Holy Spirit and with power, and because God was with him, Jesus went about doing good and curing all who had fallen into the power of the devil" (Acts 10:38). It is not necessarily a blessing to be sick – to be healed is. Although we can grow closer to the Lord through sickness, it is because of God's favour alone that draws us through the sickness into wholeness.

The innocent suffer from social evils such as war and famine, from the negative effects of the sins of the parents or ancestors, and even from the effect of their own sin or foolishness or that of others. Unnecessary pain, hardship, sickness, suffering are the result of sin in the world whether from original sin, the ever-increasing weight of all sin ever committed or personal sin. Sickness, suffering and death result from sin's entry into the world which was created good. God's desire, will and outreach are to bring healing and wholeness, to save all from sin and death.

9. May the laity use blessed oil in praying for the sick?

There are two kinds of blessed oil: one is used in the administration of sacraments by bishop, priest or deacon; the other is used as a sacramental by the laity. The olive oil used in the sacraments is normally blessed by the bishop of a diocese at the annual Chrism Mass prior to the celebration of Easter. The oil used by the laity can be blessed by any priest, the oil being set aside for sacred purpose as a sacramental. As one may use holy water or blessed salt, so one may use blessed olive oil in praying with the sick. An anointing with the blessed oil is given on the forehead or hands or both, either silently or accompanied by prayer. This oil is often called the "oil of gladness." There is a longstanding tradition of oil being used by lay people for blessing the sick. Brother André of St. Joseph's Oratory Shrine in Montreal, Quebec, was well-known for his distribution of what he called "St. Joseph's Oil" to be used for the sick. Blessed oil is also available in many places and shrines such as the Holy Sepulchre in Jerusalem.

Some people regularly use blessed oil in praying for the sick, others do not. Some use holy water. Others simply lay hands lightly on those receiving prayer as they pray for their needs. Whichever form or combination is used, the key is to bring the one receiving prayer to the point of having expectant faith and trust in Jesus the Healer. It is not necessary to use blessed oil, but it is a sign of the strength of the Spirit being imparted for healing of the sick.

10. What about the phenomenon of "resting in the Spirit"?

Resting in the Spirit, also known as being "slain in the Spirit" or being "overwhelmed with the Spirit," is a phenomenon that occurs frequently when people receive prayer. Those who experience it feel immersed or bathed in the Lord's love, feel completely relaxed and rise feeling wonderfully refreshed. Frequently occurring in large groups of people receiving prayer, it certainly captures the attention of people while being frightening to some and resisted by many. I certainly don't know why or how it happens, but those who experience it sense an invisible pressure forcing them to the ground. The pressure may be felt on the head, shoulders or behind the knees. The recipient remains completely conscious but unable to move while the experience is happening. It lasts usually a few minutes but may be much longer, an hour or two. During this experience, the person may receive healing, a prophetic message, a clear direction, an answer to a problem, a blessing. It has frequently been called the Lord's own anaesthetic while He does the necessary surgery, as it were.

Personally, I used to preach against this until it happened to me, and I could not doubt my experience. While some may fake the experience or give it undue attention or importance, it, nevertheless, is a valid sign of God's direct action. It is also a great help in ministry, especially when there are many to receive prayer – it allows those offering prayer to move quickly through a large number of people.

Certainly, the pages of the Scriptures offer similar incidents of people falling to the ground when confronted by the Lord, such as John 18:6, where those arresting Jesus fell to the ground; Acts 9:4, where under God's power Saul fell to the ground; and Daniel 10:9, where Daniel falls to the ground at the sound of the angel's voice. The experience of God's love, power and presence can be overwhelming to any mortal. As with any spiritual experience, it is authentic and a blessing when it is a work of God, but is harmful and destructive when people are manipulated, emotionally worked up or are deliberately pushed or forced over. The phenomenon bears good fruit when it is authentically the work of God.

Chapter 10

THE CHALLENGE AND PLACE OF HEALING IN EVANGELIZATION TODAY

In Haiti, in 1981, Pope John Paul II spoke for the first time about the "new evangelization" so needed in the world today – an evangelization of the baptized. So many knew the importance of the sacraments but not the Gospel; so many of the baptized were not following faithfully the way of the Church, the way of faith. Calling for a proclamation of the Gospel that would reach people in new ways so that they could understand and respond to the love of Jesus and the offer of salvation, he was seeking to have the heart of the Church renewed.

On May 31, 1998, Pope John Paul II spoke to a major gathering of renewal movements in Rome:

> In Jerusalem, almost 2,000 years ago, on the day of Pentecost, before an astonished and mocking crowd, due to the unexplainable change observed in the Apostles, Peter courageously proclaims: "Jesus of Nazareth, a man attested by God ... you crucified and killed by the hands of lawless men. But God raised him up" (Acts 2:22-24). Peter's words expressed the Church's self-awareness, based on the certainty that Jesus Christ is alive, is working in the present and changes life.

> The Holy Spirit, already at work in the creation of the world and in the Old Covenant, reveals himself in the Incarnation and the Paschal Mystery of the Son of God, and in a way "burst out" at Pentecost to extend the mission of Christ the Lord in time and space. The Spirit thus makes the Church a stream of new life that flows through the history of mankind.

> With the Second Vatican Council, the Comforter

89

recently gave the Church, which according to the Fathers is the place "where the Spirit flourishes,"[26] a renewed Pentecost instilling a new and unforeseen dynamism.

Whenever the Spirit intervenes, He leaves people astonished. He brings about events of amazing newness, He radically changes people and history. This was the unforgettable experience of the Second Vatican Ecumenical Council, during which, under the guidance of the same Spirit, the Church rediscovered the charismatic dimension as one of her constitutive elements: "it is not only through the sacraments and the ministries of the Church that the Holy Spirit makes holy the people, leads them and enriches them with His virtues. Allotting His gifts according as He wills (cf. 1 Corinthians 12:11), He also distributes special graces among the faithful of every rank ... He makes them fit and ready to undertake various tasks and offices for the renewal and building up of the Church."[27]

Today I would like to cry out to all of you gathered here in St. Peter's Square and to all Christians: Open yourselves docilely to the gifts of the Spirit! Accept gratefully and obediently the charisms which the Spirit never ceases to bestow on us! Do not forget that every charism is given for the common good, that is, for the benefit of the whole Church.[28]

Among the many charisms of the Spirit, the charism of healing is greatly needed in the Church today. So many people look for hope, strength, peace and healing in their lives. They are looking for Jesus and need witnesses who are able to lead them to encounter Him. The power of the Spirit present in the mainline churches does not seem to be evident and many search elsewhere to have their hunger and their needs met. The new evangelization is often accompanied by signs and wonders, healings and miracles, changed hearts and lives as people experience their own personal Pentecost and the Lord's ongoing ministry to bring them to wholeness, holiness.

Yet, there are many who doubt the possibility of God's intervention for healing and many who try to block His action, attributing healing to delusion, the demonic or simple hysteria or over-emotionalism. Some simply dismiss the Lord's healing action as not possible, denying the possibility of belief, and others that the sick person was not really sick but only thought they were.

St. Paul, writing to the Corinthians, reminds that: "In my speeches and the sermons I gave, there were none of the arguments that belong to philosophy; only a demonstration of the power of the Spirit. And I did this so that your faith should not depend on human philosophy but on the power of God" (1 Corinthians 2:4-5). There is power in the Gospel being proclaimed and demonstrated as Paul witnessed about Jesus as the crucified Christ. The new evangelization relies on the demonstration of power, the charisms of the Spirit being manifested through those who believe and witness to Jesus.

How did Jesus evangelize? "He went around the whole of Galilee teaching in their synagogues, proclaiming the Good News of the kingdom and curing all kinds of diseases and sickness among the people. His fame spread throughout Syria and those who were suffering from diseases and painful complaints of one kind or another, the possessed, epileptics, the paralysed, were all brought to him, and he cured them. Large crowds followed him" (Matthew 4:23-25). Signs and wonders accompany the proclamation of the Good News. To accept and believe the Good News is to experience the power of the Gospel, the power of Jesus, the action of the Holy Spirit to bring healing and wholeness.

The Baptism in the Holy Spirit is the result of the conversion process as one turns from the way of sin, choosing life, personal relationship with Jesus as Lord and learning to depend on the Spirit who generously bestows His gifts to empower and enable the believer to live the Christian life, the way of love. The charisms are tools that serve the building up

91

and the strengthening of the Body of Christ to operate in faith.

So many Christians are sacramentalized but not evangelized. Even the evangelizer regularly stands in need of being evangelized at a deeper level. Ongoing conversion of heart and life and life-style are necessary for the Christian to steadfastly follow Jesus in the power of the Spirit. Everywhere Christians need to be catechized in the power of the Spirit. Where it is being done, the people embracing conversion of heart grow and mature in the faith. Where it is not, people remain unaware of the heritage, the blessing and the power that is theirs by virtue of their baptism.

The Holy Spirit is the principal agent of renewal. The work of conversion is the work of the Spirit. It is the Spirit who reveals Jesus to us, reminds us of all He has done and taught. It is the Spirit who gives wisdom and insight, clarity and direction to all who are receptive to His guidance and empowering. To have a life of prayer and a healthy self-criticism can keep one on the right track.

Healing is a wondrous tool in evangelization today. Healing prayer is being used where the Word of God is proclaimed. People are healed and set free, renewed and experience change in heart, life and relationships. In developing countries, the use of healing prayer together with evangelism is a major factor in the drawing of and conversion of people to Jesus Christ. Healing prayer is also a reason for the meteoric increase of the charismatic and Pentecostal churches in the past century.

Healing prayer ministry is for those who are hurting spiritually, emotionally, physically, psychologically. It is direct and personal prayer for the one who is hurting and it is often accompanied with the laying on of hands (and/or an anointing with blessed oil). This prayer offered with expectant faith witnesses significant healing or improvement in a person's condition by the power of the Holy Spirit. This can happen immediately as the prayer is being offered and the healing may be so complete that the person is cured of their ailment.

Jesus trained his group of twelve apostles to evangelize, sending them out as Luke records: "He gave them power and authority to drive out all demons and to cure diseases, and he sent them out to preach the kingdom of God and to heal the sick" (Luke 9:1-2). Again, He sent out another seventy-two to evangelize, telling them, "Heal the sick who are there and tell them, 'The kingdom of God is near you'" (Luke 10:9).

The Good News is that Jesus is alive and He heals today. Filled with compassion He reaches out to His people who will receive His healing and blessing through the Spirit. We should pray for the sick and distressed on every appropriate occasion, whenever people are willing to receive prayer in their need. We should pray not only for the healing of believers but also for the unbelievers that they will be healed and come to full faith in Jesus the Lord.

It is the living Jesus with whom people experience a heart response that brings about change of heart, transformation, real spiritual growth, healing of hurts and freedom of spirit. A cognitive response to Jesus is simply not enough; it does not give inner peace and joy. The Lord and His love are real, not just theory. Jesus is a living person and when people encounter Him they are changed and are no longer the same once they know and experience that the Lord of all creation lives within them.

The Church through the Second Vatican Council encouraged the use of the charisms for evangelization, for the renewal and increasing expansion of the Church. In *Lumen Gentium* 12, Pope John Paul II wrote: "These charisms, even though extraordinary, should be received with thanks and great joy."

In an article written by Matteo Calisi in September 2001 the author writes:

To support the use of this ministry of healing in the Catholic Church, the Vatican expressed itself on three important occasions:

(a) The first is a report edited by four Vatican Dicastries which affirms that: special attention should be reserved to the dimension of experience, that is, the discovery of the person of Christ through prayer and a dutiful life (for example, in the Charismatic renewal and the other movements the experience of being "born again"). Special attention should be given to the ministry of healing through prayer.[29]

(b) The second document is a letter from the Vatican's Secretary of State, in the name of John Paul II, to the participants in the International seminar on the ministry of healing organized by International Catholic Charismatic Renewal Services (ICCRS) at San Giovanni Rotondo (Foggia) in October 1995: "His Holiness trusts that the Seminar will contribute to the further appreciation of the charismatic gifts of healing in their essential aspect in relation to the faith in Christ and the building up of His Church in unity and love."

(c) The third document was recently published by the Congregation for the Doctrine of Faith entitled "Instruction for prayer to receive healing from God."[30]

The Pontifical Council for the Laity of the Vatican invited ICCRS to collaborate in the organization of a Colloquium to be held in Rome on the topic of "Prayer for Healing and the Catholic Charismatic Renewal in the Catholic Church." The colloquium was held in November 2001, and brought together bishops, cardinals, theologians, specialists and renewal leaders to explore the ministry of healing in the Catholic Church. The phenomenon of divine healing is being addressed by the Church and one day we will see the healing ministry of Jesus Christ being exercised in every church throughout the world. We live in hope to see that day when all people turn to Jesus for healing, wholeness and holiness. In the meantime, we continue to pray, to study and call forth what we believe – the healing ministry of Jesus Christ is continuing in the Church today, setting captives free, making whole the People of God, calling forth the faith necessary to believe as the Good News is proclaimed that Jesus is alive!

END NOTES

1. Eusebius, *Ecclesiastical History 3*, Loeb Classical Library, 1. 309, as quoted by R. A. N. Kydd, *Healing through the Centuries*, (Hendrickson, 1998), p. 20.

2. A. Cleveland Coxe, *The Ante-Nicene Fathers*, Vols. 1, 3-6, (Grand Rapids, MI: Eerdmans, 1951).

3. Iranaeus, *Adv Haer* 2: 32, as quoted by Michael Green, *Evangelism in the Early Church*, (Hodder and Stoughton, 1970), p. 190.

4. Tertullian, *To Scapala*, Chapter 5, as quoted by A. Cleveland Coxe, *The Ante-Nicene Fathers*, Vol. 3: 107, (Grand Rapids, MI: Eerdmans, 1951).

5. Novation, *Treatise Concerning the Trinity*, Chapter 29, as quoted by A. Cleveland Coxe, *The Ante-Nicene Fathers*, Vol. 5: 641.

6. Origen, *Contra Celsus*, translated by H. Chadwick, (Cambridge University Press, 1965), p. 450.

7. *Apostolic Constitutions*, c. A.D. 375, as quoted by Michael Green, *Evangelism in the Early Church*, (Hodder and Stoughton, 1970), p. 192.

8. John Paul II, *Lumen Gentium 11*, cf. James 5:14-16; Romans 8:17; Colossians 1:24; 2 Timothy 2:11-12; 1 Peter 4:13, as quoted in *Catechism of the Catholic Church*, 1499.

9. 2 Corinthians 12:9 and Colossians 1:24, as quoted in *Catechism of the Catholic Church,* 1508.

10. cf. John 6:54-58 and 1 Corinthians 11:30, as quoted in *Catechism of the Catholic Church,* 1509.

11. cf. Council of Constantinople II (553): DS 216; Council of Florence (1439): 1324-1325; Council of Trent (1551) 1695-1696, 1716-1717, as quoted in *Catechism of the Catholic Church,* 1510.

12. Council of Trent (1551): DS 1695; cf. Mark 6:13; James 5:14-15, as quoted in *Catechism of the Catholic Church,* 1511.

13. Council of Trent (1551): DS 1696, as quoted in *Catechism of the Catholic Church,* 1512.

14. Paul VI, *Apostolic Constitution*, "Sacram Unctionem Infirmorum," November 30, 1972.

15. Council of Trent (1551): DS 1694, as quoted in *Catechism of the Catholic Church,* 1523.

16. R. A. Lambourne, *Community, Church and Healing,* (London: Darton, Longman and Todd, 1963), Chapter 8, as quoted by Leo Thomas, O.P. and Jan Alkine, *Healing as a Parish Ministry, Mending Body, Mind, and Spirit,* (Notre Dame, IN: Ave Maria Press, 1992), Chapter 1, Endnote 10.

17. *Catechism of the Catholic Church,* 798.

18. *Ibid.,* 799.

19. *Ibid.,* 800.

20. Oreste Pesare, "Ongoing Healing through Pastoral Care," in *International Catholic Charismatic Renewal Services (ICCRS) Newsletter*, Vol. XXVII, 6, November-December 2001. Vatican City.

21. Joseph Bernardin, *In Service of One Another; Pastoral Letter on Ministry*, (Chicago: The Chicago Catholic Publishing Co., 1985).

22. Luke Timothy Johnson, *Religious Experience in Earliest Christianity*, (Minneapolis, MN: Fortress Press, 1998), p. 182, 184.

23. *Ibid.*, pp. 61-64.

24. *Ibid.*, pp. 65-67.

25. *Ibid.*, p. 68.

26. *Catechism of the Catholic Church*, 749.

27. John Paul II, *Lumen Gentium* 12, November 21, 1964.

28. John Paul II, "The Church expects from you the 'mature' fruits of communion and commitment." Message at the meeting between Pope John Paul II and the ecclesial movements and new communities in St. Peter's Square, Rome, May 30, 1998, in *L'Osservatore Romano*, weekly edition, (English version), June 3, 1998.

29. Edizioni Dehoniane, *The Phenomenon of Sects and New Religious Movements, a Pastoral Challenge*, (Bologna: 1986), Chapter 3.3, as quoted by Matteo Calisi, "The Ministry of Healing in the Catholic Church," in *ICCRS Newsletter*, September-October 2001.

30. Matteo Calisi, "The Ministry of Healing in the Catholic Church," in *ICCRS Newsletter*, September-October 2001.

BIBLIOGRAPHY

Books

A Time to Heal: A Contribution Towards the Ministry of Healing. Report for the House of Bishops on the Healing Ministry. London: Church House Publishing, 2000.

A Time to Heal: The Development of Good Practice in the Healing Ministry: A Handbook. Report for the House of Bishops. London: Church House Publishing, 2000.

Ashbook, James B. *Paul Tillich in Conversation.* Graduate Theological Foundation: Wyndham Hall Press, 1988.

Bernardin, Joseph. *In Service of One Another; Pastoral Letter on Ministry.* Chicago: The Chicago Catholic Publishing Co., 1985.

Bosworth, F. F. *Christ the Healer.* Tarrytown, NY: Fleming H. Revell Co., 1973.

Catechism of the Catholic Church. Ottawa: Publications Service, Canadian Conference of Catholic Bishops, 1994.

Coughlin, P. B., (ed.) *He's Alive! Personal Stories of Faith, Conversion and Renewal.* Hamilton, ON: C.C.S.O. Bread of Life Renewal Centre, 2000.

------. (ed.) *He's Alive! Volume II, More Personal Stories of Faith, Conversion and Renewal.* Hamilton, ON: C.C.S.O. Bread of Life Renewal Centre, 2001.

------. *Understanding the Charismatic Gifts*. Hamilton, ON: C.C.S.O. Bread of Life Renewal Centre, 1998.

------. *The Fire in My Heart*. Hamilton, ON: C.C.S.O. Bread of Life Renewal Centre, 1998.

Coxe, A. Cleveland. *The Ante-Nicene Fathers*, Vols. 1, 3-6. Grand Rapids, MI: Eerdmans, 1951.

Dalby, Gordon. *Healing the Masculine Soul*. Dallas, TX: Word Publishing, 1988.

DeGrandis, Robert, S.S.J. with Linda Schubert. *Resting in the Spirit*. 1989.

Dinolfo, John. *A Place of Healing: The Virgin Mary in Medjugorje*. Toronto: Ave Maria Centre of Peace, 2001.

Dossey, Larry, M.D. *Healing Words: The Power of Prayer and The Practice of Medicine*. San Francisco: Harper, 1993.

Dunkerley, Don. *Healing Evangelism*. Grand Rapids, MI: Chosen Books, 1995.

Fellows Yearbook. Donaldson, IN: Graduate Theological Foundation, 2000.

Gesy, Lawrence, M.Div. M.S. *The Hem of His Garment – True Stories of Healing*. Huntington, IN: Our Sunday Visitor, 1996.

Green, Michael. *Evangelism in the Early Church*, Hodder and Stoughton, 1970.

Hampsch, John H., C.M.F. *Healing Your Family Tree.*
Huntington, IN: Our Sunday Visitor, Inc., 1989.

------. *The Healing Power of the Eucharist.* Ann Arbor, MI: Servant
Publications, 1999.

Harpur, Tom. *The Uncommon Touch: An Investigation of Spiritual
Healing.* Toronto: McClelland & Stewart, Inc., 1994.

Hart, Archibald D. *Healing Life's Hidden Addictions: Overcoming
the Closet Compulsions That Waste Your Time and Control
Your Life.* Ann Arbor, MI: Servant Publications, 1990.

Hofinger, Johannes, S.J. *Pastoral Life in the Power of The Spirit.*
New York: Alba House, 1982.

Jerusalem Bible. Garden City, NY: Doubleday & Company, Inc.,
1966.

John Paul II. *Lumen Gentium* 12, 1964.

Johnson, Luke Timothy. *Religious Experience in Earliest
Christianity.* Minneapolis, MN: Fortress Press, 1998.

Kelsey, Morton T. *The Cross: Meditations on the Seven Last Words
of Christ.* New York: Paulist Press, 1980.

------. *Healing and Christianity: a classic study.* Minneapolis, MN:
Augsburg, 1995.

Kydd, Ronald A. N. *Healing Through the Centuries: Models for
Understanding.* Peabody, MA: Hendrickson Publishers,
1998.

MacMullen, Ramsay. *Christianizing the Roman Empire (AD 100–400)*. New Haven, CT: Yale University Press, 1984.

MacNutt, Francis, O.P. *Healing, Revised and Expanded – The Bestselling Classic*. Notre Dame, IN: Ave Maria Press, 1999.

------. *Overcome By the Spirit: The Extraordinary Phenomenon That is Happening to Ordinary People*. Grand Rapids, MI: Chosen Books, 1990.

------. *The Power to Heal*. Notre Dame, IN: Ave Maria Press, 1977.

Matthews, Dale A., M.D. with Connie Clark. *The Faith Factor: Proof of the Healing Power of Prayer*. New York: Viking, 1998.

Meehan, Bridget, S.S.C. D.Min. *The Healing Power of Prayer*. Liguori, MO: Liguori, 1988.

Miner, Malcolm H. *Healing is For Real*. New York: Morehouse-Barlow Co., 1976.

Origen. *Contra Celsus*. Translated by H. Chadwick. Cambridge University Press, 1965.

Paul VI. *Apostolic Constitution*, "Sacram Unctionem Infirmorum." November 30, 1972.

Pearson, Mark A. *Christian Healing: A Practical and Comprehensive Guide*. Grand Rapids, MI: Chosen Books, 1995.

Rolheiser, Ronald. *The Holy Longing: The Search for a Christian Spirituality*. New York: Doubleday, 1999.

Roth, Ron. *Healing, Wholeness and Holiness: Touching God's Mercy.* Peoria, IL, 1989.

Ryan, Barbara Shlemon. *Healing Prayer: Spiritual Pathways to Health and Wellness.* Ann Arbor, MI: Servant Publications, 2001.

Thomas, Leo, O.P. and Jan Alkire. *Healing As a Parish Ministry: Mending Body, Mind, and Spirit.* Notre Dame, IN: Ave Maria Press, 1992.

Thomas, Zach. *Healing Touch: The Church's Forgotten Language.* Louisville, KY: Westminster/John Knox Press, 1994.

Wicks, Robert J. *Touching the Holy: Ordinariness, Self-Esteem, and Friendship.* Notre Dame, IN: Ave Maria Press, 1992.

Wimber, John. *Healing,* Vol. I and II. Placentia, CA: Vineyard Ministries International, 1985.

Wimber, John and Kevin Springer. *Power Points.* San Francisco: Harper, 1993.

------. *Power Healing.* San Francisco: Harper, 1991.

------. *Power Evangelism.* San Francisco: HarperCollins, 1986.

Woolmer, John. *Healing and Deliverance.* East Sussex, England: Monarch Books, 1999.

Articles

Bongers, Agnes. "Rites, rituals, reasons; Healing after Loss." *The Hamilton Spectator*, June 30, 2001.

Calisi, Matteo. "The Ministry of Healing in the Catholic Church." *International Catholic Charismatic Renewal Services (ICCRS) Newsletter*, Vatican City, Vol. 27, 5, Sept/Oct 2001.

"Call to Accept Suffering in Faith: Conferees Give a Perspective to Prayers for Healing." Healing Colloquium, Rome, Nov. 13, 2001.

Davis, Jeanie. "The Power of Prayer in Medicine: People Who Are Prayed For Fare Better." *WebMD Medical News*, Nov. 6, 2001.

"Healing Testimonies." *Divine Voice Magazine*. Kerala, India: Divine Retreat Centre, Feb. 2001.

"Instructions on Prayers for Healing." *Congregation for the Doctine of the Faith*, Sept. 14, 2000.

John Paul II. "The Church expects from you the 'mature' fruits of communion and commitment." Message at the meeting between Pope John Paul II and the ecclesial movements and new communities in St. Peter's Square, Rome, May 30, 1998. *L'Osservatore Romano*, weekly edition, (English version), June 3, 1998.

McManus, Jim, CCSR. "Healing in the Catholic Tradition." *New Creation Magazine*. Dublin, Ireland, April 2001.

Pereira, Rufus. "The Catholic Ministry of Deliverance." *ICCRS Newsletter*, Vatican City, Vol. 27, 4, July/Aug 2001.

Pesare, Oreste. "Ongoing Healing through Pastoral Care."
     ICCRS Newsletter, Vatican City, Vol. 27, 6, Nov/Dec
     2001.

Poulter, Geoff and Gina. "Ministering Healing." Healing
     Guidelines From the Vatican. *Good News Magazine*,
     London, England: Jan/Feb 2001.

"Vatican, Charismatics Discuss Prayers of Healing." Catholic
     News Service, *The Catholic Register*, Dec. 2, 2001.

APPENDIX A:
HEALING IN THE OLD TESTAMENT

1. **Genesis 20:1-18:** "God healed Abimelech, his wife and his slave girls, so that they could have children."
2. **Genesis 21:1-7:** "Sarah conceived and bore a son to Abraham in his old age, at the time God had promised."
3. **Exodus 4:1-7:** Moses "his hand covered with leprosy ... was restored, just like the rest of his flesh."
4. **Exodus 15:26:** "It is I, Yahweh, who give you healing."
5. **Exodus 21:18-19:** "Care for him until he is completely cured."
6. **Exodus 23:25:** "Worship Yahweh your God, and I ... remove sickness from among you."
7. **Leviticus 13:1-46:** Leprosy, swellings, scabs, discolorations, chronic leprosy, boils, burns, diseases of the scalp and chin, rash, loss of hair ... laws and regulations ... declared clean or unclean.
8. **Leviticus 14:1-32:** Purification of lepers.
9. **Leviticus 15:1-33:** Sexual impurities of men and women ... being made clean.
10. **Leviticus 16:29-30:** Day of Atonement. "Before Yahweh you will be clean of all your sins."
11. **Numbers 12:1-15:** Miriam, Moses' sister, healed of leprosy. "Please heal her, I beg you."
12. **Numbers 16:41-50:** Moses stops a plague among the Israelites.
13. **Numbers 21:4-9:** Healing from snakebites in the wilderness. "If anyone was bitten by a serpent, he looked at the bronze serpent and lived."
14. **Deuteronomy 7:15:** "Yahweh will keep all sickness far from you."

15. **Deuteronomy 32:29:** "It is I who deal death and live; when I have struck it is I who heal."
16. **Joshua 5:8:** "They stayed to rest in the camp till they were well again."
17. **Judges 13:2-24:** Manoah's wife healed of barrenness.
18. **1 Samuel 6:3:** The return of the ark from the Philistines. "Then you will be healed."
19. **1 Samuel 16:14-23:** "Whenever the spirit from God troubled Saul, David took the harp and played; then Saul grew calm, and recovered, and the evil spirit left him."
20. **1 Samuel 25:6:** "Peace to you, peace to your House, peace to all that is yours."
21. **1 Kings 13:4-6:** "The man of God placated Yahweh; the king's hand was restored."
22. **1 Kings 17:17-24:** "Yahweh heard the prayer of Elijah and the soul of the child returned to him and he revived."
23. **2 Kings 2:19-22:** "I make this water wholesome: neither death nor miscarriage shall come from it any more."
24. **2 Kings 4:8-37:** Elisha restores life to the son of the Shunammite woman.
25. **2 Kings 5:1-14:** Elisha heals Naaman of leprosy.
26. **2 Kings 13:21:** "The [dead] man had no sooner touched the bones of Elisha than he came to life and stood up on his feet."
27. **2 Kings 20:1-11:** Isaiah heals King Hezekiah of an ulcer and prolongs his life.
28. **2 Chronicles 7:14:** "If my people who bear my name, humble themselves, and pray and seek my presence and turn from their wicked ways, I myself will hear from heaven and forgive their sins and restore their land."
29. **2 Chronicles 20:9:** "Should calamity befall us, or war, punishment, pestilence, or famine, then we shall stand before this Temple and before you, for your name is in this Temple. From the depths of our distress we shall cry

to you, and you will hear and save us."

30. **2 Chronicles 28:15:** "Men expressly nominated for the purpose saw to the relief of the prisoners ... provided them with food, drink and shelter ... and took them back to their kinsmen."

31. **2 Chronicles 30:19-20:** "May Yahweh in his goodness cover up the fault of anyone who sets his heart to seeking God."

32. **2 Chronicles 32:24-26:** "Hezekiah fell ill and was at the point of death. He prayed to Yahweh, who heard him."

33. **Tobit 12:15:** "God sent me to heal you and your daughter-in-law Sarah."

34. **Tobit 14:3:** "After his cure he lived from then on in comfort, practicing almsgiving and continually praising God and extolling his greatness."

35. **Job 5:18:** "For he who wounds is he who soothes the sore, and the hand that hurts is the hand that heals."

36. **Psalm 6:2:** "Pity me, Yahweh, I have no strength left, heal me, my bones are in torment."

37. **Psalm 30:2:** "Yahweh, my God, I cried to you for help, and you have healed me."

38. **Psalm 30:3:** "Yahweh, you have brought my soul up from Sheol, of all those who go down to the Pit you have revived me."

39. **Psalm 34:19-20:** "Hardships in plenty beset the virtuous man, but Yahweh rescues him from them all; taking care of every bone, Yahweh will not let one be broken."

40. **Psalm 38:3:** "No soundness in my flesh now you are angry, no health in my bones because of my sin."

41. **Psalm 41:4:** "Cure me for I have sinned against you."

42. **Psalm 55:18:** "His peace can ransom me from the war being waged on me."

43. **Psalm 103:1-5:** "Bless Yahweh my soul, bless his holy name, all that is in me! Bless Yahweh, my soul, and remember all his kindnesses: in forgiving all your

offenses, in curing all your diseases, in redeeming your life from the Pit, in crowning you with love and tenderness, in filling your years with prosperity, in renewing your youth like an eagle's."

44. **Psalm 107:19-20:** "Then they called to Yahweh in their trouble and he rescued them from their sufferings; sending his word and curing them, he snatched them from the Pit."

45. **Psalm 147:2-3:** "He brought back Israel's exiles, healing their broken hearts, and binding up their wounds."

46. **Proverbs 3:7-8:** "Fear Yahweh and turn your back on evil: health-giving, this, to your body, relief to your bones."

47. **Proverbs 4:20-22:** "My son, pay attention to my words ... they are life to those who grasp them, health for the entire body."

48. **Proverbs 12:18:** "The tongue of the wise brings healing."

49. **Proverbs 13:17:** "A malicious messenger means a fall into misfortune, a trusty envoy heals."

50. **Proverbs 15:4:** "The tongue that soothes is a tree of life; the barbed tongue, a breaker of hearts."

51. **Proverbs 15:30:** "A kindly glace gives joy to the heart, good news lends strength to the bones."

52. **Proverbs 16:24:** "Kindly words are a honeycomb, sweet to the taste, wholesome to the body."

53. **Ecclesiastes 3:3:** "A time for healing."

54. **Isaiah 6:10:** "Be converted and healed."

55. **Isaiah 19:22:** "They will turn to Yahweh who will listen to them and heal them."

56. **Isaiah 30:26:** "Then moonlight will be bright as sunlight and sunlight itself seven times brighter ... on the day Yahweh dresses the wound of his people and heals the bruises his blows have left."

57. **Isaiah 32:3-4:** "The eyes of those who see will no longer be closed, the ears of those who hear will be alert, the

heart of the hasty will learn to judge, the tongue of stammerers will speak clearly."

58. **Isaiah 33:24:** "No one living there shall say, 'I am sickly'; the people who live there will be forgiven all their faults."

59. **Isaiah 35:5-6:** "Then the eyes of the blind shall be opened, the ears of the deaf unsealed, then the lame shall leap like a deer and the tongues of the dumb sing for joy."

60. **Isaiah 38:5:** "I have heard your prayer and seen your tears. I will cure you."

61. **Isaiah 38:16:** "Lord, my heart will live for you, my spirit will live for you alone. You will cure me and give me life, my suffering will turn to health."

62. **Isaiah 53:5:** "Yet he was pierced through for our faults, crushed for our sins. On him lies a punishment that brings us peace, and through his wounds we are healed."

63. **Isaiah 57:18-19:** "But I will heal him, and console him, I will comfort him to the full, both him and his afflicted fellows, bringing praise to their lips. Peace, peace to far and near, I will indeed heal him."

64. **Isaiah 58:6-8:** "Is this not the sort of fast that pleases me ... to let the oppressed go free.... Then will your light shine like the dawn and your wound be quickly healed over."

65. **Isaiah 61:1:** "He has sent me to bring good news to the poor, to bind up hearts that are broken."

66. **Jeremiah 3:22:** "I want to heal your disloyalty."

67. **Jeremiah 8:15:** "We were hoping for peace ... for the time of healing."

68. **Jeremiah 8:21-22:** "The wound of the daughter of my people wounds me too.... Is there not balm in Gilead any more? Is there no doctor there? Then why does it make no progress, this cure of the daughter of my people?"

69. **Jeremiah 14:19:** "We were hoping for peace ... for the

moment of cure."

70. **Jeremiah 17:14:** "Heal me, Yahweh, and I shall really be healed, save me, and I shall be saved, for you alone are my hope."

71. **Jeremiah 30:12-17:** "Your wound is incurable, your injury past healing ... so great is your guilt, so many your sins.... But I will restore you to health and heal your wounds – it is Yahweh who speaks."

72. **Jeremiah 33:6:** "I will hasten their recovery and their cure; I will cure them and let them know security and peace in full measure."

73. **Jeremiah 46:11:** "Go up to Gilead in search of balm.... You multiply remedies in vain, nothing can cure you."

74. **Jeremiah 51:8-9:** "Go and fetch balm for her wounds, perhaps she can be cured! – We tried to cure Babylon; she has got no better."

75. **Lamentations 2:13:** "Who can rescue and comfort you, virgin daughter of Zion? For huge as the sea is your affliction; who can possibly cure you?"

76. **Ezekiel 30:21:** "Son of man I have broken the arm of Pharaoh king of Egypt; you can see no one has bound up his wound to heal it, given it a bandage or a dressing to make the arm strong enough to wield the sword again."

77. **Ezekiel 34:4,16:** "You have failed to make weak sheep strong, or to care for the sick ones, or bandage the wounded ones. You have failed to bring back strays or look for the lost.... I shall look for the lost one, bring back the stray, bandage the wounded and make the weak strong. I shall watch over the fat and healthy. I shall be a true shepherd to them."

78. **Ezekiel 47:12:** "Along the river, on either bank, will grow every kind of fruit tree with leaves that never wither and fruit that never fails; they will bear new fruit every month, because this water comes from the

sanctuary. And their fruit will be good to eat and the leaves medicinal."

79. **Daniel 4:33-34:** "... my reason returned ... his promises are always faithfully fulfilled."

80. **Hosea 5:13, 15:** "Ephraim has seen how sick he is and Judah the extent of his wound, so Ephraim has turned to Assyria, Judah has appealed to the Great King; but he has no power to cure you nor to heal your wound ... I am going to return to my dwelling place until they confess their guilt and seek my face."

81. **Hosea 6:2:** "... he will heal us ... he will bandage our wounds."

82. **Hosea 7:1:** "Whenever I want to heal Israel I am confronted by the guilt of Ephraim and the wickedness of Samaria."

83. **Hosea 11:3:** "I took them in my arms; yet they have not understood that I was the one looking after them."

84. **Hosea 14:4:** "I will heal their disloyalty, I will love them with all my heart."

85. **Nahum 3:19:** "There is no remedy for your wound, your injury is past healing."

86. **Zechariah 11:16:** "... an incompetent shepherd.... He will not bother about the lost; he will not look for the stray; he will not heal the wounded; he will not support the weary."

87. **Malachi 4:2:** "But for you who fear my name, the sun of righteousness will shine out with healing in its rays."

88. **Ecclesiasticus 38:1-15:** "Honour the doctor with the honour that is his due in return for his services.... Healing itself comes from the Most High, like a gift from a king.... The Lord has brought medicines into existence from the earth and the sensible man will not despise them.... He uses them to heal and to relieve pain, the chemist makes up a mixture from them. Thus there is no end to his activities, and through him health extends

across the world. My son, when you are ill, do not be depressed, but pray to the Lord and he will heal you. Renounce your faults, keep your hands unsoiled, and cleanse your heart from all sin.... Then let the doctor take over – the Lord created him too – and do not let him leave you, for you need him. Sometimes success is in his hands, since they in turn will beseech the Lord to grant them the grace to relieve and to heal, that life may be saved. If a man sins in the eyes of his Maker, may he fall under the care of the doctor."

APPENDIX B:
THE HEALING MINISTRY OF JESUS

1. **Mark 1:23-25; Luke 4:33-35:** Man with an unclean spirit set free.
2. **Matthew 8:14-15; Mark 1:30-31; Luke 4:38-39:** Healing Simon's mother-in-law.
3. **Matthew 8:16-17; Mark 1:32-34; Luke 4:40-41:** Healing of many people.
4. **Mark 1:39:** Casting out devils.
5. **Matthew 8:2-4; Mark 1:40-42; Luke 5:12-13:** Healing a leper.
6. **Matthew 9:2-7; Mark 2:3-5; Luke 5:17-25:** Healing the paralytic.
7. **Matthew 12:9-13; Mark 3:1-5; Luke 6:6-10:** Healing the man with a withered hand.
8. **Matthew 12:15-16; Mark 3:10-11:** Healing the multitude.
9. **Matthew 8:28-32; Mark 5:1-13; Luke 8:26-33:** Healing the Gerasene demoniac.
10. **Matthew 9:18-19, 23-25; Mark 5:22-24, 35-43; Luke 8:41-42, 49-56:** Restoring Jairus' daughter to life.
11. **Matthew 9:20-22; Mark 5:25-34; Luke 8:43-48:** Healing the woman with issue of blood.
12. **Matthew 13:58; Mark 6:5-6:** Healing a few sick people.
13. **Matthew 14:34-36; Mark 6:55-56:** Cures at Gennesaret.
14. **Matthew 15:22-28; Mark 7:24-30:** Healing of Syrophoenician's daughter.
15. **Mark 7:32-35:** Healing the deaf and dumb man.
16. **Mark 8:22-26:** Cure of a blind man at Bethsaida.
17. **Matthew 17:14-18; Mark 9:14-27; Luke 9:38-43:** Healing the epileptic demoniac child.
18. **Matthew 20:30-34; Mark 10:46-52; Luke 18:35-43:**

Healing blind Bartimaeus.

19. **Matthew 8:5-13; Luke 7:2-10:** Healing the centurion's servant.
20. **Matthew 9:27-30:** Restoring sight to two blind men.
21. **Matthew 9:32-33:** Healing a dumb demoniac.
22. **Matthew 12:22; Luke 11:14:** Healing the blind and dumb demoniac.
23. **Matthew 4:23; Luke 6:17-19:** Healing multitudes.
24. **Matthew 9:35:** Curing all kinds of diseases and sickness.
25. **Matthew 11:4-5; Luke 7:21:** Healing multitudes.
26. **Matthew 14:14; Luke 9:11; John 6:2:** Healing large crowds.
27. **Matthew 15:30:** Healing large crowds.
28. **Matthew 19:2:** Healing large crowds.
29. **Matthew 21:14:** Healing the blind and lame in the Temple.
30. **Luke 7:11-15:** Raising the widow's son.
31. **Luke 8:2:** Healing of Mary Magdalene and other women.
32. **Luke 13:10-13:** Healing of a crippled woman on a sabbath.
33. **Luke 14:1-4:** Healing of a man with dropsy.
34. **Luke 17:11-19:** Healing of ten lepers.
35. **Luke 22:49-51:** Healing of the servant's ear.
36. **Luke 5:15:** Healing of large crowds.
37. **Luke 13:32:** Casting out devils.
38. **John 4:46-53:** Healing the nobleman's son.
39. **John 5:2-9:** Cure of a sick man at the Pool of Bethzatha.
40. **John 9:1-7:** Cure of the man born blind.
41. **John 11:1-44:** Raising Lazarus to life.
42. **Matthew 28:1-10; Mark 16:1-14; Luke 24:1-43; John 20:1-29:** Jesus raised to life on the third day.

APPENDIX C:
THE HEALING MINISTRY OF THE
DISCIPLES OF JESUS

1. **Matthew 10:1-8; Mark 3:13-19, 6:7-13; Luke 9:1:** The mission of the Twelve.
2. **Luke 10:1-24:** The mission of the seventy-two disciples.
3. **Matthew 17:14-21; Mark 9:14-17; Luke 9:37-45:** Disciples attempt to cast out demons.
4. **Matthew 16:13-20:** Power to bind and to loose.
5. **Matthew 28:16-20; Mark 16:14-20; Luke 24:44-53; Acts 1:1-11:** Mission to the world
6. **Acts 2:43:** Signs and wonders on the day of Pentecost.
7. **Acts 3:1-16:** Healing of lame beggar at the Beautiful Gate.
8. **Acts 4:23-31:** Prayer for confidence and healing signs.
9. **Acts 5:12-16:** The apostles work signs and wonders.
10. **Acts 8:4-13:** Ministry of Philip in Samaria.
11. **Acts 9:10-19:** Ananias and Saul.
12. **Acts 9:32-35:** Peter ministers healing to paralyzed Aeneas at Lydda.
13. **Acts 9:36-41:** Peter is used to restore Tabitha to life.
14. **Acts 14:3:** Paul and Barnabus minister with signs and wonders.
15. **Acts 14:8-10:** Paul ministers healing to a crippled man.
16. **Acts 14:19-20:** Paul raised at Lystra after being stoned.
17. **Acts 16:16-18:** Paul casts out an evil spirit from a young woman.
18. **Acts 19:11-12:** Healings and deliverances ministered by Paul at Ephesus.
19. **Acts 20:7-12:** Eutychus raised from the dead by Paul's prayer.

20. **Acts 28:1-6:** Paul healed from viper's bite at Malta.
21. **Acts 28:7-8:** Paul ministers healing to the father of Publius.
22. **Acts 28:9:** Paul ministers healing to other people.
23. **Galatians 3:5:** Working miracles.
24. **Hebrew 2:4:** God confirms their witness with signs and marvels and miracles.

APPENDIX D:
SCRIPTURAL PROMISES ANSWERING PRAYER

1. **Job 22:27:** "You will pray and he will hear."
2. **Psalm 34:17:** "They cry for help and Yahweh hears and rescues them from all their troubles; Yahweh is near to the broken-hearted, he helps those whose spirit is crushed."
3. **Psalm 50:14-15:** "Fulfill the vows you make to the Most High; then you can invoke me in your troubles and I will rescue you."
4. **Psalm 55:17:** "I complain, I groan; he will hear me calling."
5. **Psalm 65:2:** "Vows to you must be fulfilled, for you answer prayer."
6. **Psalm 91:14-16:** "I rescue all who cling to me, I protect whoever knows my name, I answer everyone who invokes me, I am with them when they are in trouble; I bring them safety and honour. I give them life, long and full, and show them how I can save."
7. **Psalm 145:18-19:** "Yahweh acts only out of love, standing close to all who invoke him, close to all who invoke Yahweh faithfully. Those who fear him need only to ask to be answered; he hears their cries for help and saves them."
8. **Proverbs 15:29:** "Yahweh ... listens to the prayers of the virtuous."
9. **Isaiah 30:19:** "He will be gracious to you when he hears your cry; when he hears he will answer."
10. **Isaiah 58:9:** "Cry and Yahweh will answer; call, and he will say, 'I am here.'"

11. **Isaiah 65:24:** "Long before they call I shall answer; before they stop speaking I shall have heard."
12. **Jeremiah 29:11-12:** "I know the plans I have in mind for you ... plans for peace, not disaster, reserving a future full of hope for you. Then you will call to me, and come to plead with me, I will listen to you."
13. **Jeremiah 33:3:** "Call to me and I will answer you."
14. **Zechariah 13:9:** "They will call on my name and I shall listen."
15. **Matthew 6:6:** "When you pray, go to your prayer room and, when you have shut your door, pray to your Father who is in that secret place, and your Father who sees all that is done in secret will reward you."
16. **Matthew 6:8:** "Your Father knows what you need before you ask him."
17. **Matthew 7:7-8, 11:** "Ask, and it will be given to you; search and you will find; knock, and the door will be opened to you. For the one who asks always receives; the one who searches always finds; the one who knocks will always have the door opened to him ... how much more will your Father in heaven give good things to those who ask him."
18. **Matthew 21:22:** "If you have faith, everything you ask for in prayer you will receive."
19. **Mark 11:24:** "I tell you therefore: everything you ask and pray for, believe that you have it already, and it will be yours."
20. **John 14:13, 14:** "Whatever you ask for in my name I will do, so that the Father may be glorified in the Son. If you ask for anything in my name I will do it."
21. **John 15:7:** "If you remain in me and my words remain in you, you may ask what you will and you shall get it."
22. **John 16:23-24:** "Anything you ask for from the Father he will grant in my name. Until now you have not asked for anything in my name. Ask and you will receive and so

your joy will be complete."

23. **James 5:16:** "So confess your sins to one another, and pray for one another, and this will cure you; the heartfelt prayer of a good man works powerfully."

24. **1 John 3:22:** "Whatever we ask him, we shall receive, because we keep his commandments and live the kind of life that he wants."

25. **1 John 5:14-15:** "We are quite confident that if we ask him for anything, and it is in accord with his will, he will hear us; and knowing that whatever we may ask, he hears us, we know that we have already been granted what we asked of him."

PRAYER FOR HEALING

Lord Jesus Christ, You are the Healer. All things are possible with You. Stretch out Your hand and heal. Work your Signs and wonders to bring healing to my brother (sister). Minister in the power of Your Holy Spirit to bring the fullness of healing, to meet the needs expressed as I speak Your word of authority, Your word of command.

In the name of the Lord Jesus Christ, be healed.

In the name of the Lord Jesus Christ, be set free.

In the name of the Lord Jesus Christ, come into the fullness of health and restoration, for the Father's glory, for your blessing, and for the blessing of all those you serve.

In the name of Jesus Christ be it done.

Thank you, Jesus. Praise you, Jesus. How holy is Your name.

Alleluia!

About the Author

Reverend Peter Burdette Coughlin was born in Hamilton, Ontario, Canada, on October 11, 1941. The eldest of five children, he was ordained a priest for the Hamilton diocese on June 3, 1967. He has served several parishes as an associate and as pastor, currently holding the position of pastor at St. Andrew Parish in Oakville, Ontario.

He became involved with Charismatic Renewal in 1971, finding in it a renewal of his life as a priest. In 1972 he became active in the healing ministry and has travelled extensively, teaching and ministering divine healing. Gifted in ministry and administration, he has held many positions in the Renewal, including the Diocesan Bishop's Liaison to the Renewal, Director of Service for the provincial Renewal in Ontario, the Ontario Bishops' Liaison to the Charismatic Renewal, and he has served as member, secretary and chairman of the national service committee for the Renewal in Canada.

He is the editor of *The Bread of Life* magazine, the national Charismatic Renewal magazine in Canada, of which he is the founding editor. To date he has published five books: *Understanding the Charismatic Gifts*; *The Fire in My Heart*; *He's Alive! Personal Stories of Faith, Conversion and Renewal, Volumes I and II*; and the most recent – *Explosion of Fire: Holy Spirit Ministry*, which looks at the first thirty-five years of Charismatic Renewal.

He graduated with a Masters Degree in Christian Spirituality from Creighton University in Omaha, Nebraska, in 1999 and entered the doctoral program at the Graduate Theological Foundation in Donaldson, Indiana, in the year 2000, graduating May 2, 2003.

He does his writing at his cottage beside a river where he appreciates the quiet and the beauty of the pastoral view. His greatest delight is in watching what the Lord does as he ministers to the people through word, sacrament and healing prayer. He is happy to be a priest.

How to Order

The Healing Ministry of Jesus Christ Continuing in the Church Today $10.00

Other books by the same author/editor:

Explosion of Fire: Holy Spirit Ministry $15.00

He's Alive! Volume II $15.00
More Personal Stories of Faith, Conversion and Renewal

He's Alive! Volume I $15.00
Personal Stories of Faith, Conversion and Renewal

Understanding the Charismatic Gifts $7.00

The Fire in My Heart $10.00

FOR ALL ORDERS PLEASE ADD Shipping and handling:

> $6 if one book is ordered.
> $1 for each additional book shipped in the same order.

Send cheque for full amount in Canadian funds to:

> C.C.S.O. Bread of Life Renewal Centre
> P.O. Box 395
> Hamilton, ON L8N 3H8 Canada

Bookstores

For details of trade discounts offered, please:

Call: **(905) 529-4496**
FAX: (905) 529-5373
e-mail: *info@thebreadoflife.ca*